FINANCES

The Other "F" Word

Another "F" Word to Love

by
Mel O CFP®

First Edition. NV, United States. February, 2019

www.financestheothefword.com

ISBN 978-1-7336659-2-6

EDITED BY:

amandaedens.com

FORMATING, COVER AND GRAPHICS BY:

castdesignteam.com

This book is dedicated to my best
friend, Jesse Duban. Jesse, you died too
soon, and I miss you every day. I wish
you were here for this.

I love you, my Jesse.

Table of Contents

Foreword

Ever since I can remember, way back when I was
a little girl, you know, that time of your life that
you literally can't remember past that point, I have
dreamed about being a star! But it's not about the
fame. It's the way music touches me and lifts me up
to a level that nothing else can. When I perform, I
want to share that same feeling with the audience,
to reach down and pick the crowd up, and really
connect with them. When I was 5 years old, I sang
"I'm Gettin' Nuttin' For Christmas" in my elementary
schools' holiday play, and I was hooked! I wanted
more, and I didn't care how, whether I sang, danced,
or played an instrument. I LOVE to entertain. It's the
most intoxicating feeling I have ever experienced.

I grew up listening to country music, but when I was a
teen, I heard rock n roll for the first time and was never
the same again! I bought an electric guitar, learned
every rock song I could, and formed and played in
several all-girl bands. My first one was an all-girl heavy
metal band called Killer Instinct, and I played rhythm
guitar. It didn't take long before I was progressing as
a guitarist and wanted to play lead, so I moved on
to my next one, also all girls, called Bootleg. We had
a recording deal with RCA Records, and I recorded
my first EP. Both these bands were based in L.A.

Then, in 2003, after moving to Las Vegas, NV., I formed Jaggedy Ann, an explosive all girl rock band. In 2006 we recorded an album called "Boiling Point", which was produced by drummer, Phil Rudd, of the legendary AC/DC. We went on two huge world tours.

The band was on the verge of becoming something really big. Everything was amazing, but, unfortunately, before the album was even released, at the end of our 2007 tour, we were notified that our label filed bankruptcy, and that our album, our rights, etc., were being handed over to a new company. We were not prepared, and this led to financial devastation for everyone involved.

After that, I struggled, hard, as a single mother, until I was lucky enough to meet my rescuer, who I married, and then everything was great!

Then, in 2011, four years later, "Boiling Point" was released worldwide. By then, we had lost momentum, and everyone had moved on. We still haven't seen a single dime of revenue, as the "new" record label is still recouping. Something we never thought would happen.

Since then, I decided to never let myself be put in that situation again, and I took control of my musician life. I started being more proactive about the business aspect about it. Because, let's face it, we musicians play music because something grabbed us and took hold of our hearts, made us want to devote our entire lives to making music and bringing joy to those who we touch with our songs.

We do it because we love it, even when it's not fruitful, which is sadly, 90% of the time. It's feast or famine. Sometimes it's good and other times it's not. Sometimes gigs are abundant and the other half of the time there's nothing. We also make friends with our bandmates, and close relationships form, just from the sheer love of doing something so passionate together, making it hard to separate friendship from business.

So, how do you take something you love, something that's so much fun, and amazingly fulfilling, something you can't live without, and turn it into a "business"?

Let's face it, I am incredibly lucky to have the gift of songwriting and the natural ability and love of performing, but most musicians, like myself are almost entirely passion driven. We think with our hearts and are willing to put EVERYTHING on the line to pursue our dream, regardless of the financial impact and repercussions of making reckless, soul driven decisions. I am great at the creative part, writing, recording, performing, etc., but I really struggle with the "business" side of things. I must constantly remind myself to be mindful of it.

I have a little sticky note on my bathroom mirror that says, "Be a smart business woman". It's there to remind me every day, when I want to take a gig that I know I'm not only not going to make money, but it's going to cost me money. It's there to remind me to not give away merch for free to everyone who is a "friend". It's there to remind me not to party after a show, then feel all hung over the next day, instead, go to bed, wake up feeling good and get to the gym and take care of myself so I can continue to do this thing that I love so much. It's there to remind me to fully read contracts and hire a lawyer if I don't understand it. It's there to remind me that I am a boss lady and I am responsible for my own destiny.

So, I try to stay smart, but at the end of the day, I am, and will always be, just a musician intoxicated by the feeling that playing my music gives to me. That's why having Mel O to help guide me through the financial stuff is so helpful.

I just finished reading her book on finances and man, it made me feel even more grateful to her.

She manages to take all the major finance topics and break them down so that they are easy to understand, even for a right brained person like me. She also uses rock and roll lingo to help explain things, and you know that helped ME out a lot.

Believe it or not, the book is even kind of sexy here and there (I'll let you see for yourself what I mean by that!).

This is definitely a new and exciting time for me. I find so much inspiration and things to write about just in my everyday life alone. In fact, it's the very portal of expressing my most intimate feelings that I could not otherwise. I write about everything that is important or has affected me in some way or another.

No matter who you are, what you do, but especially if you're a right brained, "I do it because I love it" kind of musician, like me, you will find lots of useful information in this book. And, regardless of whether you are already very financially literate or if you are just a beginner.

Thanks Mel, and rock on sister!

Love,
Leona Xoxo | www.leonaxrocks.com

"Performing, for me, is like a drug that gets me high, one that you never tried. It's like flying to outer space and becoming a shooting star, soaring through the sky. It takes me 6 hours to come down after a show!"- Leo

Introduction

Greetings new tribe member and may I commend you for purchasing a book written by someone named Mel O - yes, that is my actual name, and it should be noted there is no period at the end of it. I call you a tribe member because we are all part of the same clan: the money clan. We eat, breathe, and wallow in money, and it is the biggest contributor to our culture; just listen to any song. Whether you love or loath money, you are nonetheless in the money game. By reading this book, you are now in my Hot Moon Tribe, and I say welcome to the fold. So, who am I, and why did I write this book? More importantly, why should you devote time out of your life that you'll never get back to read it? All good questions; walk with me.

I am a Certified Financial Planner™, or a cooler way to say it is CFP®. In addition to that, I hold a Series 7, Series 66, and a Health and Life license. More importantly than that, I am a rocker chick through and through. I have stage dived, moshed (getting my ass kicked thoroughly), and still make the rock sign every chance I get.

\m/

Boom, see you've just been rock signed.

However, I am also good at money (written purposely that way so chill out grammar Nazis) and explaining how to understand it. If **#music** and **#money** are both important to your life, then you've found your MECCA.

I wrote this book because lots of people in my industry tell you what you can't do: you can't retire at 55, you can't buy that, blah, blah, blah. No wonder people hate us. However, minor tweaks in your portfolio and budgeting can lead to a life fuller of the fun stuff: time with friends, travel, investment income and humanitarian work. But you must understand the basics of how money works and how it can make more money for you. This is what we will discuss in this book. Also, to prep you, I have Attention Deficit Disorder - SQUIRREL. I am not an author, so I wrote this book as a way to have an unfiltered conversation with you about money. Also, as I write, I will be constantly interrupting myself with asides. Sorry I'm an Xer and my attention span was ruined by MTV. For my Millennial bros and sisters, that was when MTV actually played music, unlike whatever crap they air now.

Now, this is a very, VERY important aside. A lot of people out there represent themselves as Financial Advisors or worse yet Financial Planners, when in fact they are insurance agents. This is the deal;

---

insurance policies are one of the highest payers in our industry and quite frankly not one of the hardest licenses to get (in my opinion). Because of this you have tons of people getting licensed and then being TOLD they are financial advisors and financial planners. They then go forth and spew it to the world. Please for F sake make sure you know who you are speaking with. Insurance is a vital part of a financial plan, but it is NOT YOUR WHOLE PLAN.

If it sounds like I'm knocking insurance agents, sorry; as Gene Simmons says "feel free to send your hate mail to my PO Box."

Now, back to the intro.

I started investing at 18 and realized that the "rich" people made money because they understood money. My grandparents who raised me were Great Depression children, and they hardly spent a dime. They put their money in CDs and Savings accounts, and that is as far as they went. In my opinion, their retirement stunk. They didn't travel; they didn't do anything but watch the weather (seriously look out a window) and the news ALL day. It sucked for me to see that, and I knew that I was going to work in finance to avoid being like them.

I want you, tribe member, to make and understand
money, and ENJOY your money and I don't
want to put you to sleep while learning how to
do so. Life is too short, and we never know if
we will wake up tomorrow. Read this book to
take back your time and your enjoyment.

Also, if you don't know by now, I am not an old
white guy in a suit, like most others in my industry,
so I will not be speaking like one. Buckle up
your ears buckaroos it's going to get bumpy.

Introducing

Ozzy

If you got 'em, he'll
smoke 'em.

Slagathor

The color black isn't
dark enough for him.

Blokie

When you throw your
panties, he will catch them.

Papi D

He likes gold chains,
reggaeton, and "sexy gatas"

1

Where Do You Start?

Financial Jargon

*"Money, it's a hit / Don't give me
that goody good bullshit"*

\- Pink Floyd

from **"Money"** off ***Dark Side of the Moon*** released in 1973

In order to start speaking the language of money you need to understand the language. A lot of times, the only knowledge people have of investing is their 401ks or simply how to pronounce "401k". They often speak of their 401k like the investment, so when I ask them something like, "How much knowledge do you have about investing?" they often reply, "Oh, you mean like 401ks? Yeah, I know about them." The 401k is not the investment; it is the account. Is this confusing? You'll understand soon enough. So let's start with some basic terminology.

Checking Account (FDIC Account)

An account designed typically to pay bills or temporarily house liquid money. It usually pays zero to little interest and utilizes a VISA check card to facilitate spending. If you are new to the finances game, please understand that a VISA check card does NOT build your credit. It is simply a tool for you to access your funds quickly and easily. As a recommendation for you, do not keep large amounts of money in your checking account. In the event you are a victim of fraud (not a Victim of Changes like Judas Priest), you will have turned over the keys to a ton of money for the fraudster. Typically, in events of fraud, banks will refund your money, but this is a process and could take some time. Bottom line, don't make things easy for criminals. Oh, and for God's sake, do not use the last four (XXX-XX-1234) of your social security for your pin number. SMH, the bank can change your ATM pin number in a branch. Also, it is pronounced "checking", not "checkings and savings". I would hear that 100 times a day, and I would want to murder people's faces.

Savings (FDIC Account)

Savings accounts are accounts people use to park their emergency fund money. Make sure you read that as "fund," not "fun," money. We will discuss emergency funds and their importance in the budgeting section. Savings accounts pay interest. You might be wondering why a bank would pay you interest to put your money in their bank. When banks lend money out to customers, they are allowed to lend money based on parameters in relation to their money on deposit, specifically in CDs and savings accounts. The more the bank has on deposit, the more money they can usually lend. One of the ways a bank makes money is by lending money out and charging interest on the loaned funds. Bank's interest rates are based on the prime rate. The prime rate is the best rate a bank customer can get (this is where the title of prime and sub-prime mortgages come from, reviewed later in the book). When banks pay interest on an account they take the prime rate minus a spread; in turn, when they lend money to someone, they take the prime rate plus a spread.

Example:

PRIME RATE   **YOUR RATE EXAMPLE**

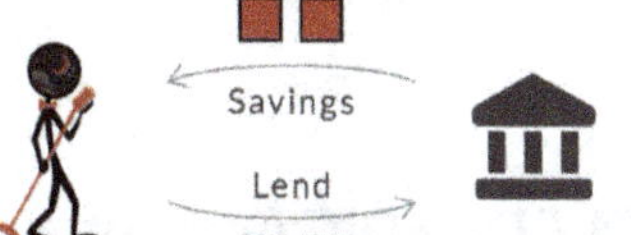

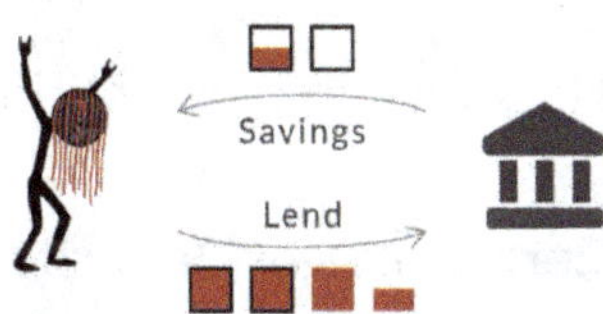

If prime is 2.00%, the bank might pay you 0.50% on money you hold in a savings account and then lend you money at 3.50%. The spread is the difference on either side a (-1.50%) for paying interest on savings and a (+1.50%)

above prime for lending money out.

Basically, banks are double dipping; they pay you less on savings and pocket the difference, and then they charge you more when they lend to you and pocket the difference. Big institutions are often recipients of loans at prime, unfortunately not us little guys.

Without going down the rabbit hole too much, the prime rate is based on the Fed (short for Federal Reserve) funds rate. To qualify for FDIC insurance, banks need to have a certain amount of money on "deposit" with the Fed at all times. Sometimes banks are short, so they borrow money from each other overnight to satisfy the FDIC balance requirements. The interest rate at which they borrow money from each other is known as the Fed funds rate, and the prime rate is based off that.

Holy fuck that was boring.

Certificates of Deposits AKA CDs (FDIC Account)

Think of a time capsule: you put stuff in it, and later, say in a couple years, you open it and see what's inside. CDs work similarly to this. A bank customer puts money into a CD for a period of time, and in exchange for that, most times banks pay you a higher interest rate than a savings account.

If you open the capsule before the set time period, the bank will assess you a penalty fee. At the end of the holding period, you receive the money you put into the CD back plus the interest it earned while it sat there. CDs can be short term, shorter than 12 months or long term, longer than 12 months.

FDIC Insurance

Anytime you go into your local bank, you will see the FDIC sign everywhere.

FDIC stands for Federal Deposit Insurance Corporation. FDIC insured accounts are typically checking, savings, and CDs. Most investments are not FDIC insured. The FDIC was created as part of the "New Deal" by FDR (Franklin Delano Roosevelt) to give people reassurances that they wouldn't lose all their money if the banking system failed again like it did during the Great Depression. Initially, FDIC insurance covered accounts up to $100,000.00 after the financial crisis in 2008; this amount was increased to $250,000.00, where it still stands today. Simply put, if you have money in a bank and the bank goes under, the Federal Deposit Insurance Corporation will reimburse your money dollar for dollar up to $250,000.00. After the Great Depression, people didn't trust the banking system, and to encourage people to return to it, they needed to provide assurance for them.

Now I am not an expert on the Great Depression but here is a super slimmed down version of what happened. At the beginning of the Great Depression, in the late '20s, banks would hold people's paper stock certificates (explained later) in their vaults. Part of what happened was that banks would "borrow" their customers stock certificates and play the market during the day and return the stock certificates to their vaults at night, the bank customers being none the wiser. This was all fine and good until the economy started grinding to a halt and the market crashed. Banks lost their clients' stocks in the market and couldn't replace them. In addition to that, people panicked and "ran" to the banks to withdraw all their money. The banks simply didn't have the money on hand nor the stocks to replace what they "borrowed" and closed their doors calling it a "bank holiday."

In reality, banks were playing the stock market with peoples' deposited money, so when the market failed, they failed too.

Crowd at New York's American Union Bank during a bank run early in the Great Depression. The Bank opened in 1917 and went out of business on June 30, 1931.

If you want a cool example of this, watch *It's a Wonderful Life.* George and Mary were on their way

to their honeymoon when they see a line forming
in front of the Baily Building & Loan. That was how
I imagined a "run" on the bank might have looked.
This is a great scene filled with panic, but of course
George Bailey, always the cool cat, calms the crowd
with his rugged sensibility and completely screws his
wife out of a decent honeymoon. Just sayin.' Now,
am I over simplifying this? Sure, I am, but we haven't
got all day. Former Fed Chair Allen Greenspan is
an expert on the Great Depression; he wrote books
on it. Knock yourself out if you can get through
them. As an aside to this *The Simpsons* does a great
revamping of this classic scene from *It's a Wonderful
Life.* Go on YouTube and search under "Simpsons
run on the bank," and you'll laugh your ass off.

If you don't know what the "New Deal"
is or who "FDR" is, then Google that shit,
and let's hope we never see another Great
Depression in either of our lifetimes.

Interest/Interest Rate/Yield/Dividend

When a bank pays you money on your money,
the difference is called interest. The percentage
at which they pay you that money is called the
interest rate. When interest is earned by you the
customer, it is quoted as annual percentage yield
(APY); if you are borrowing money, the interest

is quoted as annual percentage rate (APR).

Simply put, if you buy a $1,000.00 CD with a 12-month term (holding period) and the CD pays 3% APY (the interest rate), you would expect to earn $30.00 (the interest dollars earned) in interest on your initial $1,000.00.

Sometimes banks will 'trick' you by saying they have a 9-month CD with a 3.00% APY. See what they did there? They quote you an APY based on you holding the money with them for 12 months. However, the CD's term is only for 9 months. So, in reality you are getting less than a 3.00% APY because the money is only on deposit for 9 months not the 12 months the APY is quoted on. —"Don't hate them because they're beautiful"—for my 80's kids, you know what commercial I am referring to.

For an investment, the above holds true. However, the interest is typically replaced by the word "dividend." A dividend is the actual dollar amount that is paid out to a stock holder if applicable. The yield is the dividend paid per each share of stock divided by its value. So, for instance, if you make $0.20 cents per quarter ($0.20 * 4=$0.80) and the stock is valued at $22.00 per share, then ($0.80/$22.00= 3.63% yield). So, in this case, your divided is $0.80 cents

per year while your yield is 3.63%. Investments
are not FDIC insured. If you are looking for a
great resource check out www.investopedia.
com; it is a great website of financial terms.

Bank Accounts vs. Investments

Investment is a generic term used for anything
from a home or gold coins to mutual funds and
stocks. However, in most circles, when you use the
word investment, you are referring to a non-FDIC
insured product i.e. not a checking, savings, or CD.

Portfolio

A term used to reference any investments you hold
whether in stocks, bonds, or real estate and so on.

Common Stocks

A share of stock represents ownership in a company,
each person owning a small sliver of said company.
Some stocks have a yield and pay dividends, and
some do not. Stocks are typically riskier, and
money is made or lost when the stock is sold.
Stocks are an important part of a person's portfolio,
and although older people often benefit from stock
exposure, stocks are generally owned by younger
people. Stocks are designed for growth, and

stock holders are usually the last to get paid if the company you own goes bankrupt. A stock's price can fluctuate widely throughout the day; therefore, they are more appealing to younger people who have a longer time frame to recover from a loss.

Preferred Stocks

Preferred stocks come in two varieties: cumulative and non-cumulative. The names represent how the dividends are paid or, better yet, how they are made up if the company suspends them due to financial hardships. It is important to state that preferred stocks do NOT give ownership or voting rights. We discuss these later.

Penny Stock

Rule of thumb: penny stock is a stock that's share price is under $5.00; however, when people refer to penny stock, they often mean stock that is $2.00 or less a share.

Stock Certificate

This is the old way of holding stocks. The number of shares or "ownership" you had in a company was printed on a colorful piece of paper (refer back to my Great Depression snidbit). While they are typically beautiful documents, they are a pain in the ass (severe eye roll) to process and can be easily damaged or destroyed. If you lost or damaged your stock certificate, you would have to send away for new ones or be assed out. Thank God these are almost completely gone. Currently, shares are most often held in an account with a broker/dealer, also known as being held in "Street Name." When positions are held in "Street Name," that means that they aren't represented on a piece of paper like a stock certificate but are just reflected as ownership held in your investment account.

Mutual Funds

This is by far the most common term used when discussing investments. Think of a whole bunch of investments bundled together and then sliced up. That is a mutual fund, we discuss this in detail later.

Mutual Fund Load

Ha, why did I just read that as sounding X-rated? But I digress.

This is what we call the fee paid to get in or out of a mutual fund. Also noted, it is an album by Metallica. Some say this is when they sold out. I say that they have redeemed themselves nicely after enduring two

Load and *Reload* albums, and we are forever grateful.

Bonds

Bonds are considered "fixed income." That term is relevant because when I refer to an investment as "fixed income" later in the book, you know what I'm talking about. If you own a bond, you are a bond holder; we cover this in more detail later.

Bonds are most commonly issued
in $1,000.00 increments.

Bond Coupon Rate

The original percentage assigned to a bond at issuance. This reflects what the bond will yield. Remember the term "fixed income."

Diversified/Diversification

A tricky bugger, this simply means holding more than at least one investment i.e. being diversified. Do two different holdings make you diversified? Technically yes, but in my world, no.

Behavioral Finance

The actions you take based on a feeling

you have such as fear or greed. Fear makes people run from the market when it is tumbling and buy high when the market is climbing. We discuss this in a later chapter.

Maturity

The length of time it takes for a bond holder (you) to receive your principal (initial investment) back from a company (them). This of course is assuming the bond is purchased at issue and not on the secondary market—we cover this later.

Inflation

The price of everything going up; that's it in a nutshell.

There are many, many other ways to invest, but the big four are stocks, bonds, mutual funds, and FDIC insured products.

There is also another big four: Metallica, Anthrax, Slayer (SLAYER, it must always be screamed for some reason), and Megadeth. If only dealing with money was as awesome as being a Rockstar. <Sigh> a nerd can dream.

Now, dear tribe member, let me break down
some legal things right now. Investments
are not FDIC insured; they could lose
value and are not guaranteed.

Great info, Mel! You had me at "hello" until you
mentioned the part that I could lose my money.
So why on earth would I ever be stupid enough to
invest? Because you're stupid like a fox, that's why.

2

Stocks

The Sexy Stiletto

*"Believe me sweetie / I got enough
to feed the needy"*

- Notorious B.I.G

from **"Big Poppa'"** off ***Ready to Die*** released in 1994

As previously stated, stocks represent a slice of ownership of a company and most often have voting rights. Voting rights might seem of little importance, but if your stake in a company is large enough, your votes (1 per share of stock) could allow you to change policy at a company you are invested in. Remember the movie *Mr. Deeds* from 2002 when Adam Sandler's character Mr. Deeds stormed into the shareholders meeting to prevent the sale of Blake Media? He was granted the right to speak because he held one share of stock in the company, thus he owned a fraction of the company and was able to vote. I like to think of stocks as a sexy stiletto heel. They are aggressive and sexy, and if you catch them at the wrong time, you could break your ankle. For guys, I guess it would be new Nikes or a sexy car, you know, dude stuff. Bro-out; it's cool.

Stocks are exciting and can be prone to nice jumps in price and alternatively sharp declines. Therefore, typically you find younger people with more exposure to stocks in their portfolios, like 30-year old women and younger, wearing more high heels. Depending on market trends, a company can be IN one day and on the way OUT the next.

The difference between what you purchased a stock for vs what you sell it for is your gain or loss, and this is the primary way people make money from stocks. Sometimes stocks take a long time to get a solid return; other times, you get lucky, and returns come faster. Could you lose all your money investing in stocks? Sure, although it is typically rare.

When we discuss common stock, there are certain things we need to look at. For instance, how large is the company you are investing in? It is not a stretch to assume a startup company in comparison to Apple will have less financial stability. So, when it comes to stocks (not like the other times we tell ourselves), size does matter. Who am I kidding, size always matters.

Cap size is the measuring stick we use to measure company size from an investor standpoint. It is also one of the largest factors that differ one stock from the next. Cap is short for capitalization.

Cap	=	number of outstanding shares	X	their share price

So if you own stock in Mel's Yoga Pants, and I currently have 10,000 outstanding shares of stock for purchase on the open market at $15.00 a share, my capitalization would be $150,000.

10,000	X	**$15**	=	**$150,000**
outstanding shares		per share		Cap

Typically Cap sizes break down like this:

SIZE	MARKET CAP
Micro Caps	Up to 3 MM (million)
Small Caps	3MM - 2B (billion)
Mid-Caps	2B - 5B
Large Caps	More than 10B
Mega Caps	100B or higher

As an aside, there are a lot of big name companies such as Airbnb that are privately held. This means that the ownership of the company is held by a handful of owners and is not for sale in the market place. When a company is going "public," that is when they are allowing the public (you and me) to purchase shares and have some ownership in the company. This is done by issuing an IPO aka initial public offering. Most of you might remember when Facebook went public in 2012. All it means is that they made the transition from privately held (by the few) to publicly held (by the many). When issuing an IPO, companies must be careful when estimating how much to sell the initial shares for. A company only makes money from the IPO or the first time they release the shares to market. Once the stock is in the hands of you and me, any gain or loss is recognized by us, not the company. Businesses often go public when they need cash or to benefit financially from regulatory changes.

Depending on the advisor, the range of Cap numbers above can change slightly from each size to the next. To explain Cap size and the difference in risk between them, let's look at an example in another way.

Let's say I owned a record store named Your Mom Records (hipsters have probably listened to records "ironically." It's interesting I don't seem to see the same nostalgia for tapes). I must remind you that this is just an example, so don't take this example as gospel. Also, there is a ton of hurdles that need to be jumped in order to be listed on an exchange (covered later), but we will imagine for now that they don't exist.

Your Mom Records Location (1):
Micro Cap / Small Cap

I opened a brand-new record store, I own the store, and I probably work there from open to close every day. For the most part, I am a one man show; I probably have either no employees or very few employees.

To be honest, I could be sleeping on the floor of the store and eating Top Ramen.

Every dime I make goes back into the business for marketing, materials, longer hours to stay open, advertising, product development, etc. My cash flow is super tight. If you invest in my company, I typically can't pay you anything (yield) for investing in me because all my money is tied up in Your Mom.

Changing markets (retail and otherwise), a slowing economy, or technology could put me out of business. Day to day is how I roll. I am a small cap, I am riskier than stocks larger than me. However, you like me, and you believe in my store or product, so you take a chance on me and hope I grow into the next Amazon. As I grow, you plan to grow with me and receive a gain on your investment.

Your Mom Records Locations (5):
Mid Cap

I now own 5 of "Your Moms." We are still in growth mode. I am pulling out a small salary from Your Mom, but most all my dollars are going back into the business.

I have employees now and am adding more when needed. My cash flow is slightly better. I am moving through my growth cycle.

I may or may not be able to pay you, as an investor, a yield on your investment. I am less risky than small cap me, but I am not out of the woods yet. Regulations and changing markets can still severely harm my business, and my cash reserves are modest but hopefully building.

Your Mom Locations Worldwide (Everywhere):

Large Cap / Mega Cap

Everyone all over the world wants a piece of Your Mom. As the founder, I am retired on an island with a nice island boy (over 21 since I do loves my drink), and I have strangers running my company. I get a fat check, and Your Mom sells herself. Now, I can give you, as one of my investors, growth (typically slower than previously) with a little bit of a yield to boot (covered later).

I have enough of a product line to weather most changing trends, and I have a fat balance sheet in case times get tough. I have lobbying power, which means that I can bully or buy out some of my competition. In addition, I can manipulate the formation of laws and rules in my favor or stem the tide of regulation changes that negatively affect me. I am less risky than mid cap me because of how long I've been in business, and my market reach is "yyuuugggge."

When companies get to this size monopoly rules come into play. Monopoly rules are designed to make sure that one specific company doesn't have too far of a reach that it can stop or block out competition.

Do monopoly rules really work, or is that just BS Mel? Let's say this nicely: ask Google and Amazon.

Now depending on where you are in your life, at any given time, you can have some of these cap sizes or all of these cap sizes in your portfolio. The stock portfolio will depend on what you need at the time and what your goals are. If you are about to retire while growth is still important, you don't typically take the same amount of risk as when you were young and building your wealth.

As stated, we have been discussing common stocks. There are many other types of stocks, but for simplicity (and boredom), we will cover only two additional ones here: **preferred stocks** and **penny stocks.**

While common stock is the most "common"

type of stock, we now shift to preferred stocks, lovingly called preferreds for short.

Preferred stock is kind of in between common stock and fixed income. For those of you who fear commitment, this might be your jam. A preferred stock does not have voting rights and typically trades very near $25.00 per share. Preferreds typically pay a quarterly dividend and, for the most part, do not have wild fluctuations. 2008 was the exception to this rule like many others and is covered in a later chapter.

Preferreds in most cases pay a higher yield (dividend) than common stock. Common stock may pay a dividend or not, but preferreds always pay dividends unless suspended (read on and it'll explain itself). People purchase preferred stock because they would like to have some upside potential while getting a better yield compared to common stock. Preferred stocks are also usually more liquid than bonds.

There are two types of preferred stock: **Cumulative** and **Non-Cumulative.** If you own a preferred cumulative stock, it means that if the company decides to suspend its quarterly dividends, you get your back payments first before the business can reinstate the dividends for everyone else. To put it differently, if you hold a non-cumulative preferred stock, you will begin receiving dividend payments again, but you are assed out on the ones the company suspended for the entire time they suspended them.

Check the example below of a preferred stock paying a dividend of $1.00 per share per quarter (3-month period).

QUARTER		NON CUMULATIVE	CUMULATIVE
1		$ 1.00	$ 1.00
2		$ 1.00	$ 1.00
3	Dividend suspended	$ 0.00	$ 0.00
4	Dividend renewed	$ 1.00	$ 2.00
TOTAL		$ 3.00	$ 4.00

From this example, we see that a cumulative preferred would be more appealing to an investor to own than a non-cumulative preferred because you know any missed dividends will be eventually made up. Due to this fact, cumulative preferreds typically hold their value better than non-cumulative preferreds. Preferreds are mostly purchased for their dividend, so knowing you will receive your payments is pretty important. Dividend payments are usually the most important reason people own preferred stocks.

Penny Stocks, UGH, Penny Stocks.

Penny stocks are one of the banes of my existence, not because they are bad but because of the behavioral finance behind them. Penny stocks are stocks with a share price of less than $5.00, but usually when people discuss penny stocks they mean stocks less than $2.00 a share. This low share price drives risk adverse people to make stupid, stupid mistakes. Let's say you only have $3,000.00 to invest. I am selling candy at $1,000.00 per piece, and you purchase 3 pieces of candy. You might feel pretty foolish because you only purchased 3 pieces of candy for $3,000.00. However, if I am selling candy for a penny each and you give me $3,000.00 and I give you 3,000 pieces of candy, you might feel pretty good about yourself. But in the end, people, you spent the same $3,000.00. Such is the penny stock mentality. If we substitute candy for a share of stock, we can either own 3 shares of stock or 3,000 shares of stock. Penny stocks are risky investments, and I cannot tell you how many times people will tell me they don't want to lose their money and in the same breath ask about penny stock. In the end, a shitty stock purchase is a shitty stock purchase.

Regardless if you lose your ass on 3 shares of stock vs 3,000 shares of stock, you still lost your ass. However, somehow people "feel" better purchasing more stock regardless of the quality. In the end, people don't want to lose their money, so they equate a larger quantity of stock with better quality stock, and they lose said ass referenced above.

Look, I live in Vegas, and no one understands this mentality more than casinos. Walk through any casino and see the hordes of people dumping money into penny machines vs quarter machines. If you spend $3,000.00 on a penny machine vs a quarter machine, you have still spent $3,000.00. In the casino world, gamblers believe that if they play the penny slots, even though they might still lose their money, they will be able to play longer. I go back to the prior sentence, you still spent $3,000.00 either way; the only difference is your perception. It is important to note that Vegas is smarter than you, and with all the multipliers and pay lines, a spin on a penny machine can often cost you way more than $0.25. They are banking on your behavioral finance, and they more often than not WIN. Those casinos aren't monuments to winners!

An important thing to note on penny stocks is that there is limited trading volume. Let's say you decide you want to get out of your penny stock. Well, since penny stocks are "Pink Sheets," there could be limited or no buyers for your stock at the time you want to sell. No buyers equals no sells of your stock, and you are stuck with it until there is a buyer or the stock goes to $0.00.

In closing, when thinking of penny stock reference, the cap sizes, and their associated risk above,

---

I will say it again; a shitty stock is a shitty stock regardless of how many shares of it you own.

If you still disagree with me about penny stock, then do your thing. Believe me, there are many thousands of people in my profession who will be happy to facilitate your buys into the hottest penny stock and not always with your best interest at heart.

Your CFP® can help guide you to an appropriate portfolio mix that matches your risk tolerance and goals. If you don't have a CFP®, I happen to know one. Just sayin'.

3
—

Bonds
A Discussion

In this chapter:

Slagathor
Mel's Diner Owner
and Bond Issuer

"Believe in all the good things / That money just can't buy / Then you won't get no bellyache / From eatin' humble pie"

- Aerosmith

from **"Eat the Rich'"** off *Get A Grip* released in 1993

Papi D
Original Bond Buyer

Ozzy
2nd Bond Buyer

Ahh the comfy sweater. What do you mean a comfy sweater? Well, think of your oldest, most worn-out sweater you wear. It makes you feel warm and fuzzy... and safe, like a Cosby sweater before the unpleasantness. While bonds aren't FDIC insured, they still offer the bond buyer a feeling of security. They are considered a more conservative investment for the most part (see below), and they are known as a haven from a turbulent market.

There are many different bonds and bond issuers. There are bonds issued by the federal government known as Treasury bonds, and muni bonds issued by municipalities such as water work companies, and then there are corporate bonds issued by companies. Of course, there are several more bonds out there, but Good Lord, we aren't writing the Bible here. For the sake of time and my sanity (and probably yours), we will focus on corporate bonds below.

This is how a bond works. Let's say I opened "Mel's Diner" (a lot of you don't get how awesome that joke is; it's from an old show called *Alice*, and my name is Mel—get it? But I digress).

Mel's Diner needs to build a warehouse to store its food and supplies, etc. Mel's can typically do a couple things to fund its warehouse: self-fund it themselves, go to the bank and beg them for money, or under the right circumstances (all regulated by the Securities Exchange Commission or SEC), go to Wall Street and sell a bond.

Bonds have these basic parts: face value, selling price of the bond, the bond coupon, and the bond yield. In our next example, the face value of the bond is $1,000.00, and the coupon is 6.00%.

Let's say Mel's needs $1,000,000.00 to fund their warehouse. Mel's would issue a total of 1,000 bonds at $1,000.00 each ($1,000.00 X 1,000 = $1,000,000.00). When you buy Mel's bond instead of owing money to a bank, Mel now owes money to you, the bond holder. Mel's Diner's bond has a maturity of 10 years (see definition in Chapter 1).

As a bond issuer, you give Mel's Diner $1,000.00, and they give you 1 bond. Every year you hold the bond, Mel's will pay you $60.00 ($1,000.00 X 6%=$60.00). At the end of 10 years, Mel's gives you your last annual payment of $60.00 and returns the face value of the bond ($1,000.00) to you, and the transaction is complete.

Between the issue date and maturity of the bond, one would expect that the selling price of the bond would always be $1,000.00, equivalent to the face value of the bond. Not so. As often is the way with everything, your bond would have fluctuated in price, and this is normal. At any point in time, you can have a bond that is selling at a discount, meaning its value is worth less than the initial $1,000.00 you bought it for, or you can have a bond selling at a premium where the bond's selling price is higher than the $1,000.00 you bought it for. Just think of it this way: You have an old car made in 1992 (this is BS because that's the year I graduated, whatever), and you own the car in 2009. People might laugh at you, and the car is probably worth nothing in 2009. Now fast forward to 2018 and the car is a classic and could have increased in value.

Okay, let's go through this slow. Currently, interest rates are still rather low, which means that if my company wants to borrow money from a bank, it should be able to get a lower loan rate.

If Mel's Diner is issuing a bond right now

(remember Mel is paying you the bondholder to

lend them money), would issue the bond at only say 2.50% coupon rate based on current low interest

rates, meaning that the bond buyer is only

getting 2.50% interest payment for letting borrow their money. Remember, in this scenario, as the bondholder, you are taking the place of the bank and lending a company money.

Now assume someone else is holding a bond that has a yield of 6.00%. If you are looking for a good

income stream, would you rather buy bond

at 6.00% coupon or bond at 2.50% coupon? Would it be safe to assume that you would desire the 6.00% bond yield over the 2.50% bond yield? Would a bond buyer be willing to pay a little more (a premium price) for a bond to be the recipient of a 6.00% yield vs a 2.50% yield? How many questions can I ask in a row? The answer most often to the bond question is yes, and that is when the selling price of a bond becomes higher than its $1,000.00 face value.

Now assume that a bond had a maturity of 20 years when you purchased it but there were only 5 years left on the bond until it matured (so 15 years have already passed), AND it had a 6.00% yield. Now how excited are you to buy that bond? F-ing ecstatic because the bond will mature in only 5 years, and you would be making 3.50% (6.00%-2.50%) over prevailing interest rates. Wouldn't a bond buyer pay an even higher price for that bond? Absolutely! This my friend is called buying a bond at a premium. Any dollar amount paid over the face value of a bond is considered a premium.

Now understand, just because you paid $1,100.00 for a bond that has a face value of only $1,000.00 doesn't mean that you receive $1,100.00 back at maturity. The issuer of the bond only originally borrowed $1,000.00 from , so they only are required to pay back $1,000.00. You, my friend, eat the $100.00 difference.

Think of your bond as a teeter-totter with face value price on the left and coupon rate on the right.

When the bond is purchased new, the teeter-totter is in total equilibrium. However, as market conditions change, your bond changes value, and that affects your yield even though your coupon stays the same. Huh?

So, you have a newly issued bond at $1,000.00 with a coupon of 6.00% and a yield at 6.00%. Everything is equal at issuance, your teeter-totter is perfectly balanced.

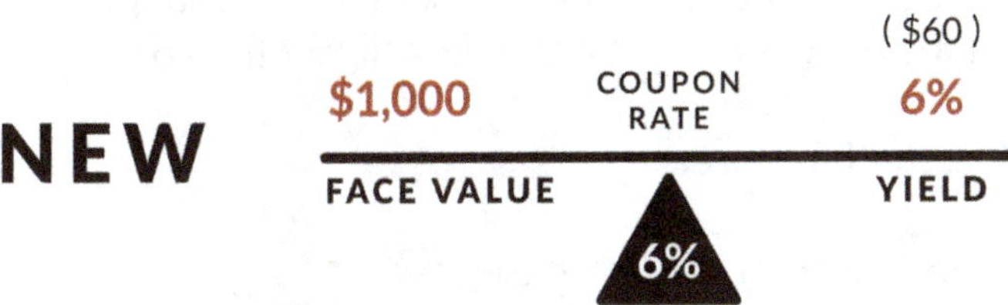

Then markets conditions start to move and change. The market factors make your bond less valuable, so your bond is only worth $890.00 instead of the $1,000.00 you paid for it.

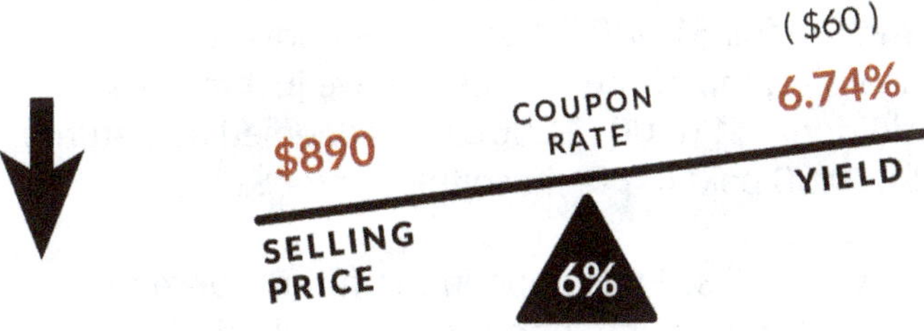

I come in and buy your bond from you for $890.00; the bond coupon is still 6.00%, but my yield is now

---

6.74%. Hang with me here; I own the bond now, and I still get paid the $60.00 annual interest (6.00% coupon on $1,000.00 face value). However, instead of buying the bond like you did for $1,000.00, I purchased it for $890.00. As a result, I paid less but still receive the $60.00 interest annually. Therefore, the coupon on the bond is 6%, but my yield is higher than 6%.

The math is here:

Purchase price of bond After issuance	**$890.00**	
Face Value of Bond	**$1,000.00**	**60 / 890 = 0.0674** or 6.74%
Bond Interest Payment Annually	**$60.00** ($1,000.00 X 6.00%)	

So the coupon is 6.00% while my yield is 6.74%.

AND, of course, if I hold the bond to maturity, I get the full $1,000.00 back at maturity, which means on top of the interest, I have just made an additional $110.00 ($1,000.00 redeemed at maturity -$890.00 paid to purchase the bond= $110.00).

Now could I sell this bond in the future for more money? Maybe; it depends on the market, the bond supply, maturity, and yield. If there is a buyer, you can usually buy or sell a bond at any time.

Now same scenario with a premium priced bond.

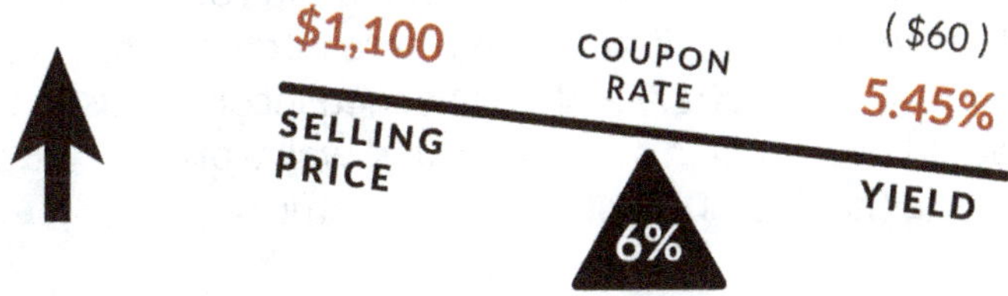

The coupon is still at 6.00%, but because I paid an additional $100.00 for the bond, I take less away in yield. Look at the teeter-totter picture above, and you'll get it.

The math is here:

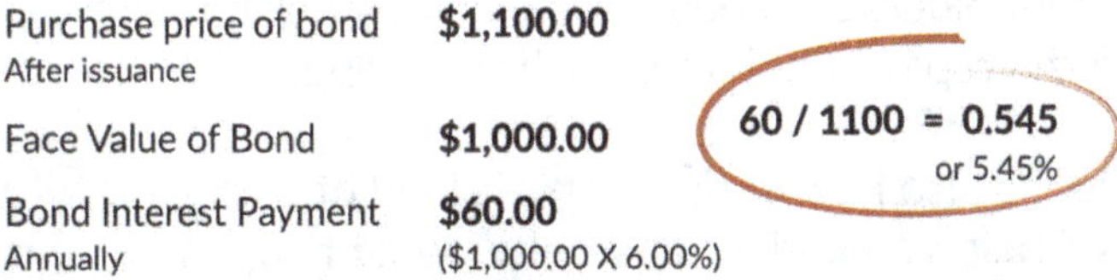

Purchase price of bond After issuance	$1,100.00	
Face Value of Bond	$1,000.00	60 / 1100 = 0.545 or 5.45%
Bond Interest Payment Annually	$60.00 ($1,000.00 X 6.00%)	

At maturity, I receive back the face value of the bond at $1,000.00 and eat the premium payment of the additional $100.00.

That sounds like the shittiest deal ever. Not only do you pay more for the bond, you also get less at maturity and less yield than the bond coupon. All true; however, if in a time where interest rates are low (2007-2017) and you needed income, this would have been a sweet deal and well worth eating the $100.00 at the bond's maturity.

Shit, I need a drink; that's a lot.

Bonds are predominantly used to anchor a portfolio in a market storm or when income needs to be injected into a portfolio. Most bonds are considered "conservative" investments. Does that mean you can't lose money? Hell no, I didn't say that; did you say that? If Mel's Diner goes out of business, you could get pennies on the dollar for your investment or nothing at all. However, bondholders are ahead of common stock holders in the repayment hierarchy if that happens.

Bonds also have ratings. This is kind of tricky and will help you understand better what happened in 2008 when you get to that chapter. Bond ratings are not regulated by the government but instead by private companies. The most popular being Moody's, Standard and Poors, and Fitch. These companies have proprietary ways they rate their bonds and only make the ratings themselves public but not how they come to the rating conclusions.

A quick aside, this is the same way credit works: Transunion, Equifax, and Experian are all private companies with their own proprietary formulas on how they calculate your credit score. This (and other factors) is why your credit score can change day by day. But that, my friends, is for another time and another book. (I am laughing my ass off right now because instead of typing 'and,' I typed 'nad,' which I do frequently, and it's always funny. Ha! Nad).

According to this rating system, some bonds are considered "investment grade", and others are considered "high-yield". Now, am I oversimplifying? Yes, there are like 15 different bond ratings which I won't go into here; you're welcome. In the 80s, they called "high-yield" bonds "junk bonds," but the word junk doesn't sound as appealing as "high-yield". Want to buy my junk guitar, my junk car, my junk dog? No thanks, bro, I'll pass. So needless to say, the name was changed from junk bonds to high-yield Bonds. Often people will tell you they invest in "high yield" bonds to sound impressive, but now you know better. High-yield bonds are lower rated bonds; thus, they have a higher yield to attract buyers, and this is where the name comes from. I am not saying these bonds are bad; it depends on your goals and risk tolerance to determine if they're right for you.

Lower bond ratings could be a result of a company's shaky financial condition or a change in market favor like what happened to cigarette companies in the mid-80s. For those of you who don't remember, in the mid-80s, Nancy Reagan was riding high on her "Just Say No" campaign, and the surgeon general was hot after the cigarette companies to add the warnings to cigarette packages you see today. A change in market caused the cigarette companies to fall out of favor. Factors such as this can affect a bond rating.

A bond can have a high rating, usually indicating strong ability of the issuer (company) to repay thus meaning less risk and lower yield for the bondholder. Higher risk vs higher return; lower risk vs lower return. Higher ratings can potentially cause the bond to sell at a premium as previously discussed. Bonds can move positive or negative through the rating systems at any time and cause a change in the selling price of the bond. While you do not need to hold a bond till maturity, the prevailing factors of when you sell or buy it will depend on the bang you get for your buck.

Also bonds that have typically longer maturities (20+ years) will fluctuate more over time than lesser maturity bonds. Think of it as a snake moving through the grass. The tip of the head will move very little; the mid-section of the snake will visibly move side to side; the tail, the longest part, will whip back and forth. Not *Wild Kingdom*, but you get the idea.

There are also many other risk factors we won't go into here. There is risk in everything you do; if you ever, EVER, evah sit down in front of someone in my industry, and they say it's no risk—quoting Monty Python—"Runaway, Runaway"—from the harmless bunny.

4

Mutual Funds

and Pizza

"Michael wants another slice"

- 5 Seconds of Summer

from **"500 years of Winter-Pizza Song"** off *She Looks So Perfect (B-Sides)* released in 2014

First off, I need to tell you there is more than one mutual fund (MF) in existence. Also, there is more than one mutual fund company. I often hear clients ask me for that (insert company name here) mutual fund, or they tell me they want the stock mutual fund. Worse is when they say that XYZ friend has XYZ fund, and they have told them how well they've done, so they want that fund. SMH, it doesn't work like that guys. There are mutual funds that hold stocks, bonds, REITS (Real Estate Investment Trusts), etc. and/or a mixture of all.

Each mutual fund company, and there are over hundreds, have several mutual funds that do this or that. There is also this weird belief that mutual funds are safer. Not true: like all non-FDIC investments, they can be conservative or risky depending on what you buy and can fluctuate and/or lose value.

MFs are diversified, but diversification doesn't mean safety. When we say diversification, we are referring to holding different types of investments from different companies or municipalities. So, if you have a portfolio with over 250 companies, someone could say you are diversified. However, if all 250 companies are in the technology sector, then the diversification isn't worth a hill of beans.

Also, many times people think they are diversified because they hold multiple mutual funds from different MF companies. So, again, I say if you have a Technology fund from Company A and a Technology fund from Company B, there is a high chance that there are the same companies' stocks being held in both mutual funds. Therefore, you are still NOT diversified. Are you picking up what I'm putting down? In 2008, I had clients who had multiple real estate properties, and guess what? They ALL lost money that year regardless of the type of real estate they owned: duplex, house, condo, etc. They weren't truly diversified.

Everyone seems to know to ask for mutual funds, but no one can ever explain to me what they are when asked. Think of an MF as a pizza.

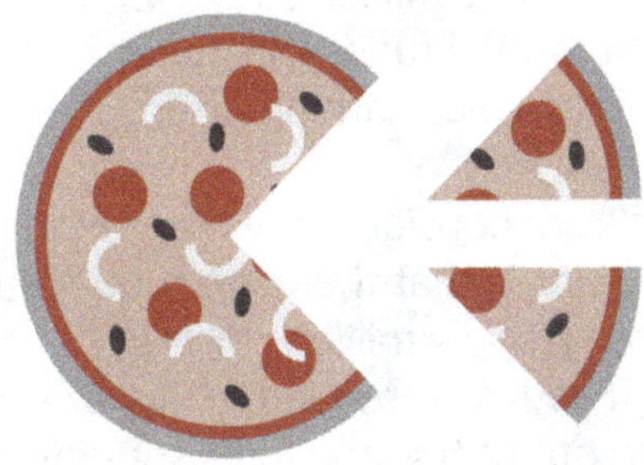

If you get a pizza with pepperoni, sausage (mmm sausage), and onions on it then split it with your friends, each of you will get a slice of said pizza. Each slice will have the same three toppings: pepperoni, sausage, and onions. Even though you each have your own individual slice, it's from the same pizza.

A mutual fund is like that. Mutual funds are made up of different financial instruments; when you buy a share of the mutual fund, you are buying a small percentage of every instrument held in that mutual fund just like getting a slice of pizza with the same toppings as everyone else. Now, you can eat more slices of pizza, which equates to buying more shares, but you will always have the same toppings on each slice while your overall consumption of pepperoni, sausage and onions will be higher. If the MF manager sells any of the stocks or buys more of a different stock, then the toppings on your pizza change.

Think of the joy you will have regaling your friends about mutual funds the next time you split a pizza—see, learning is fun.

Mutual funds are considered actively managed. What this means is that there are fund managers who oversee typically millions or billions of dollars in the fund. They may frequently buy or sell stocks/bonds in and out of the portfolio, sometimes daily, sometimes not. Due to this active management, mutual funds have 12-B1 fees, which are internal management fees, and can also have loads attached (upfront/back-end fees). Like everything, fees can range from low to high. It is important to note here that there is a misconception that if you purchase mutual funds in 401k plans, there are no fees. Bull Shit. The fees could be different, but you are still paying them, so don't kid yourself.

Let's just scratch the surface of loads. HA! Loads! There are multiple types of share classes with mutual funds, but we will only cover three of them here because, let's be honest, you don't have all day.

A Shares

This share class typically has upfront loads varying by fund and fund company in addition to lesser internal (12-B1) fees. You can sell whenever you want without penalty or fee. Also, most companies will charge less of a load on an A Share the more you invest with them. This is called hitting "breakpoints." So, someone investing $25,000.00 will typically pay more than someone investing $100,000.00 in the same fund or with the same fund company.

B Shares

Not often found any more, these are shares with no upfront load but a back-end load if a holding period is not satisfied. The holding period is usually 5-10 years, and then the B Shares will slowly convert to A Shares. However, if you sell your shares before the holding period maturity, you will be hit with a deferred load, meaning you pay money to the fund company to sell your shares or upon your exit. B Shares are often found today in some insurance policies and annuities.

C Shares

These shares have no front-end or back-end load provided you hold the shares for more than one year (366 days). In most cases, if the shares are sold within less than one year, then there is a 1.00% deferred load. These shares usually have higher internal costs, so if held for longer periods of time, they can be more expensive in the long run than its A Share counterpart.

Side note here, if you buy the ABC Stock/Bond fund in A share or C share you are still buying the same exact investments and the same exact fund (same pizza); the share classes only dictate fee structure and have their own investment qualifications.

Mutual funds also get a little weird in the way they trade. Because MFs are a soup of all types of companies or financial instruments, when sold your sell will not go through till market close. If you call me at 9 AM and say sell XYZ mutual fund, even though I place the trade at 9:01 AM, you will not technically sell out of the MF until market closes at 4 PM EST/1PM PST. So, if you call at 9 AM and the market is screaming, and after 9:01 AM the market goes in the crapper, you will get the closing price of said crapper market. In MFs, they add up all the investments in the portfolio at the close, divide it by outstanding shares, and that will be the price you receive for your share. I simplified the formula—there are other things they take into consideration—but this is the gist of it. An individual stock as previously explained sells out at the price of execution.

Pre-MF existence people had to buy individual stocks or bonds. If you didn't have a lot of money you might only be able to buy a couple shares of

stocks or a couple bonds, not a lot of diversification there. The MF was created to combat this.
This has led to the belief that MFs are a "safer" investment. Whichever MF shares you buy, there is not a guarantee that they won't lose value, therefore no share class is safer than the other.

Mutual funds are designed to do different things: some are designed to grow, some are designed to stay stable, some are speculative, etc. Consult with a professional before purchasing (hint: that would be me, tribe members, and I'll help you).

5

WTF is an ETF?

*Sorry, nobody cool sings about
ETFs, so I got nothing.*

\- Mel O CFP®

Since we spoke in detail about MFs, I think it is
only fair we discuss ETFs as well. ETF stands for
exchange-traded funds. They have some similarities
to MFs in the fact that they are comprised of
multiple companies' stocks or bonds or whatever
financial instrument in their objective. However,
they differ in many strong ways from mutual funds.

As stated previously, mutual funds are actively
managed, and the share classes in MFs contain
12-B1 fees. If someone is actively managing
your money, you pay more; that's how it goes.
ETFs are not considered actively managed.
The positions are bought and held and are only
occasionally replaced with other positions.
Because ETFs don't have daily management,
their internal fees are typically lower than MFs.

Also, when discussing ETFs, they trade the same way stocks do. If you call me at 9:00 AM PST and ask me to sell out of an ETF, and I place the trade at 9:01 AM PST, you are getting the price at that time, not the closing price at the end of the day like mutual funds.

There are a lot of companies who play in the ETF space, and many people debate whether they are a better option over MFs. This is the deal—if you think the manager knows what they are doing and can read the market, then you will lean towards MFs; however, if you think no one can predict market trends, ETFs will be a better, typically lower cost route for you to take. Which is better? Like all things, it depends; I use both depending on the situation.

Index ETFs tend to be the most popular. If you buy an Index ETF (like SPY), you will own a fraction of all the companies represented in the S&P 500 (see chapter 10). This is called index investing. Index investing can be done through an ETF or a mutual fund. Now, and let me be clear America; you are not holding an exact mirror of the S&P 500 or the Dow or other indexes. The S&P and Dow are tracking ALL the shares of said companies, and no one can own all of everything all the time.

As stated above, if you believe that no one

can read the market, you will typically be an index investor. At any given time in the market, trends can favor ETFs or MFs. However, MFs are still the most common and are the most common investments offered in 401ks.

6

Compounding

It's not just for your
weight anymore.

"The overweight lovers in the house"

- Heavy D & The Boyz

from **"The Overweight Lovers in the House"**
off ***Living Large*** released in 1987

In this chapter:

Papi D
Saving for a new car.

Okay, a quick aside, I have to tell you I love Heavy D & The Boyz. One of my favorite songs is *Now That We Found Love*. Not only is the song awesome with a cool beat, but in the video, there is a guy dancing in a see-through plastic rain suit. It's very confusing, especially because there is not one rain drop throughout the whole video. As a matter of fact, look it up on YouTube right now. Go ahead, I'll wait. I had to... just to get it out of my system. I can't imagine what the inside of that outfit was like. Ever ridden a Greyhound? But I digress; now back to the book.

Ever notice that once you gain about 5 pounds, it just kind of snowballs. Before you know it, you look at the scale, and you think how the hell did that happen? Compounding is not always a bad thing; when it comes to money, it can be your friend.

In order for you to better understand the strategies in the next chapter, you need a good understanding of the compounding concept. Easily defined, compounding is where interest earned on your initial deposit in turn earns interest. Think of this as a fruit tree that produces fruit. The fruit tree has already been paid for and the fruit it produces is extra.

Quick example:

 puts $1,000.00 into a savings account.

The savings account pays 5% APY (Annual Percentage Yield).

INITIAL INVESTMENT: $1,000.00 | 5% APY

BALANCE AFTER:

1 Year	2 Years	5 Years	10 Years	20 Years
$ 1,050.00	$ 1,102.50	$ 1,276.28	$ 1,628.89	$ 2,653.29

Now the first year had the money in the savings account, he earned $50.00. If interest was linear (sometimes referred to as simple interest) and not compounding, we would expect to continue to only earn $50.00 in interest per year making our total after 20 years only $2,000.00 ($50.00 X 20 + $1,000.00 initial investment).

However, because the interest compounds, comes to the grand total at the end of 20 years of $2,653.29.

Now look, I am not blowing your mind here (or maybe I am) because you can Google this right now. This is not new information or should not be.

But here's the deal, I am an 80's child: Reaganomics, yuppies, big hair, and bigger shoulder pads were my environment. I remember sitting in school and learning about money. The extensive knowledge they taught me about finances consisted of how to count money and how to write a check (seriously archaic by today's standards). They were raising me to be a consumer, not an investor. Compounding interest is the most powerful tool you have in your arsenal, so maybe that would have been important to teach?!

So besides compounding interest being awesome when saving money, what other practical purpose does it serve in your life? Well, for starters, guess what else compounds? Your FREAKING credit cards! Oh yeah, baby, don't think this is a one-way trip: cash, grass, or ass, nobody rides for free (also a great song by Ratt). You think that would have been nice to know before you got your first credit card? I am writing this book because I don't want you to struggle the way I did. Deep breath, Mel, chill; sorry, I get really worked up about this.

So, that means your credit card debt that is accruing interest is also accruing interest on the interest. FML. Also, guess what, boys and girls? Credit card interest compounds daily! So it will compound much faster than savings or investment earnings. With the exorbitant amount of debt that Xers and millennials typically carry, be aware of this before you purchase using credit cards, and remember this when reading the budgeting chapter.

Also, to make things saucy, interest rates change. In the last few years, we have been lucky to have low interest rates on borrowing money; however, historically this is not so. It is common for payments to increase with interest rate changes, and we are heading into an environment of raising interest rates. Borrower beware.

7

The Basics of Lending

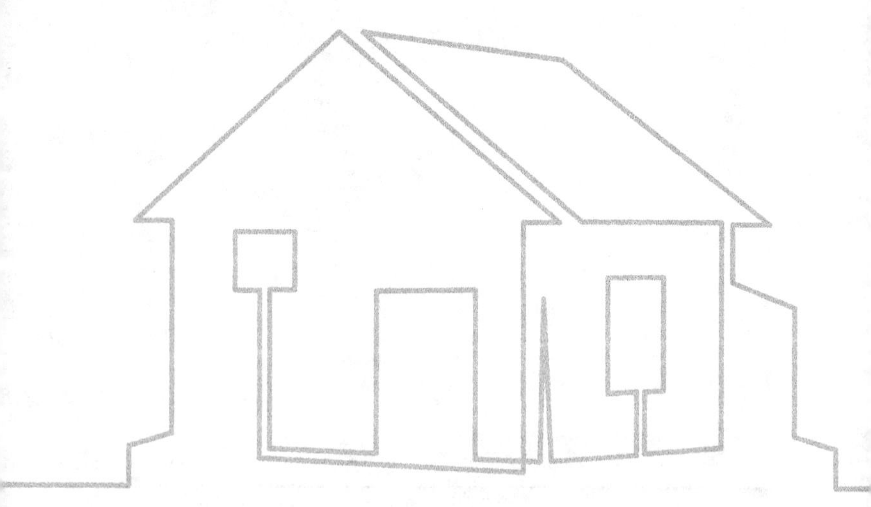

"And you have the audacity / to even come and step to me / and ask to hold some money from me / until you get your check next week"

- Destiny's Child

from **"Bills, Bills, Bills"** off *The Writing's on the Wall* released in 1999

In this chapter:

Slagathor
Buys House (15 year loan)

Ozzy
Buys House (30 year loan)

This might be the most boring chapter of the book. I apologize in advance, but there is good shit in here, so hang with me. We have been discussing compounding interest on loans and such, so let's discuss some of the different type of loans you can get.

Mortgages

This one is the most commonly known type of loan. These are used primarily to buy homes, and typical mortgages are payable over 15-30 years, also known as term or maturity. Mortgages are most often fixed with a set interest rate and set monthly payment. If you have a house payment of $1,000.00 and one month you pay $1,200.00, the next month your payment is still $1,000.00. The additional $200.00 just decreased the overall loan balance.

Another fun thing mortgages do is amortize. Let's see how to explain amortization... Remember the last chapter on compounding interest? Well, the first half of a mortgage is typically uploaded with all that interest. A better way to say is that the mortgager (bank) takes all the interest over the course of the loan term and uploads it in the first half of the mortgage.

This way, if you sell your house within the first 5-10 years, the bank has made their money back, and YOU, tribe member, still owe the balance. It's very sweet of them, right? Back in the day, this didn't matter because people bought their house, paid it off, and lived in it forever. Think of your grandparents. But in today's nomadic lifestyle with people moving around so much, this is really no longer the case.

Example

buys a house in December 2017 for $250,000.00

at 5.00% interest on a 15-year loan, and buys a home for $250,000.00 on a 30-year loan at 5.00% interest.

Now let's look at the numbers...

Purchase Price of Home (POP): $250,000.00
Loan in terms of years: 15
Balance on Loan: $250,000.00 + closing costs
Estimated Monthly Payment: $1,977.00

When	Interest	Principal/ Actual POP	Remaining Balance
1st payment	$ 1,042.00	$ 935.00	$ 249,065.00
At **5** Years	$ 777.00	$ 1,200.00	$ 185,193.00
At **10** Years	$ 437.00	$ 1,540.00	$ 103,222.00
At **15** Years	$ 8.00	$ 1,970.00	$ 0.00
At **20** Years	NA	NA	NA
At **25** Years	NA	NA	NA
At **30** Years	NA	NA	NA

Purchase Price of Home (POP): $250,000.00
Loan in terms of years: 30
Balance on Loan: $250,000.00 + closing costs
Estimated Monthly Payment: $1,342.00

When	Interest	Principal/ Actual POP	Remaining Balance
1st payment	$ 1,042.00	$ 300.00	$ 249,700.00
At **5** Years	$ 957.00	$ 386.00	$ 229,187.00
At **10** Years	$ 847.00	$ 495.00	$ 202,861.00
At **15** Years	$ 707.00	$ 635.00	$169,076.00
At **20** Years	$ 527.00	$ 815.00	$125,717.00
At **25** Years	$ 296.00	$ 1,046.00	$70,073.00
At **30** Years	$6.00	$1,340.00	$0.00

*These numbers are for example purposes only. Depending on closing cost and other finance options, they can change.

A couple things to point out here: Regardless of which loan term you picked for the first half of the loan, your monthly payment is typically going more toward the interest than the principal. Also, the 30-year mortgage's monthly payment is less because it is spread out over a longer period of time. Do you end up paying more interest over 30 years than over 15-years? You betcha. For this reason, many retirees in their last 10 years of work try like hell to pay off their mortgage before entering retirement. I will go against the grain here and say I don't think that is always the best strategy. I feel retirement should be about enjoyment as with life pre-retirement.
If having a 30-year mortgage allows you to live a better, funner lifestyle, who gives a shit if you have a mortgage? Also, in some cases, mortgage interest gives you a tax deduction (consult a tax professional). Baby boomers for the most part have all their money in IRAs and 401ks that will come out 100% taxable (see the tax chapter), and it would be nice to have the added deduction. Also, instead of paying down a mortgage like crazy, you could invest the extra money and hopefully have more income and money to enjoy in retirement. That is my two cents; well, I guess so is this whole book, but my point is still valid.

Loans and Lines of Credit

Loans and lines of credit both come in two different forms: secured and unsecured. Secured simply means the bank can take something from you if you don't pay them. Think of mortgages, car loans, motorcycle loans, etc. Typically, better rates are given on loans or lines that are considered "secured." Unsecured loans are exactly what you'd think they are; if you don't pay the bank, they have nothing to "physically" take from you. Banks can put you into collections or put a lien on your accounts, but there is no item to repo or foreclose on. Unsecured loans are often called signature loans.

A loan has a set payment at a set interest rate. Regardless of market conditions, interest rate changes, or your personal situation, you will pay the same every payment. The payments are made until the end of the term when you have completely paid off the obligation or object. If you want to buy something else or get more money, you need to apply for a new loan.

Lines of credit work similarly to a credit card, and I say that loosely. Lines of credit can be secured or unsecured. However, they are revolving, which means that—like credit cards—as you buy things and pay them down, the money becomes available for you to purchase items again. This is the major difference of a line vs a loan. The interest rate on a line of credit moves with prevailing interest rates. If rates are going up, your interest rate and payment are going up. If rates are going down, your interest and payment will typically go down as well. Lines can be dangerous if you let them get away from you (much like credit cards); however, I actually love them. They allow you the flexibility to pull down emergency money when needed and pay it down and have it there for future use.

General rule of thumb: if you have an object you want to own, then a loan is the way to go. However, if you want liquid, revolving cash and you can afford a change in payments, then lines would be a good option.

74

8

How Much Do You Like Cheese?

Inflation's Effect on Your Money

"I'm trying to make a living / I can't save a cent/It takes all of my money / Just to eat and pay my rent"

- The late, great B.B. King

from **"Inflation Blues"** off **Blues N Jazz** released in 1984

In this chapter:

Blokie
Deciding what's more important,
eating cheese today or tomorrow.

How much do you like the good cheese?

For all those out there who are lactose intolerant, my condolences. But I eat the crap out of sharp cheddar, ANY sharp cheddar.

My grandfather Papa (pronounced Paw Paw) got me hooked on sharp cheddar cheese early on. We would eat the cheese right off the block—sooo good. But there were some times when my grandparents would not buy the "good" cheese, for instance when inflation was double digits in 1979 and the early 1980's.

 As a dairy-loving kid (I mean I would literally sneak out of bed and eat heaps of butter), this really sucked. Mel, stop talking about cheese and get to the point. Sorry. Being from the Depression era, my grandparents did not believe in investing in the stock market; FDIC insured accounts were the only place they would put their money.

Sometimes their money wouldn't outpace inflation, and I would not get my cheese. #firstworldproblems

Before we get into this, let's take a quick look at the price of milk and various things throughout the years.

Year	Gallon of Gas	Milk	Basic Home
1974	$ 0.53	$ 1.39	$ 38,900.00
1984	$ 1.21	$ 2.26	$ 80,700.00
2004	$ 1.88	$ 3.00	$ 212,400.00
2014	$ 3.34	$ 3.85	$ 188,900.00

Now, as you can see by the numbers above, inflation rates go up and down throughout time. However, for the most part, inflation averages out to a steady climb. Let's look at more specific examples.

Inflation is simply the cost of things rising: cheese, travel, cars, education, health insurance, rent, etc. When putting your money in savings, you often give up potential higher returns to have your money "safe." The issue with that is typically savings, CDs, and checking accounts do not keep up with or outpace inflation. Now, I am not speaking harshly about FDIC insured accounts; they are very valuable and a big part of every financial plan, but we are speaking about inflation and its effect on your money.

Currently banks are paying anywhere from
.01% to .03% on a basic savings account
while inflation is at approximately 1.7%.

Let's work that math out to help you understand the
deteriorating force inflation has on your money.

Let's assume ☺ has $1,000.00 today, and
this $1,000.00 represents the total monies

☺ can spend on cheese for his ENTIRE lifetime.

For the purposes of simple equations, let's assume

☺ will forgo any and all cheese today

so that in 20 years' time ☺ can begin eating as

much cheese as ☺ can afford.

When ☺ relinquishes instant gratification
today for a potential return tomorrow,
that is called "opportunity cost."

Below is a chart with some ASSUMMED rates of
return. Now listen, not all savings accounts pay 1%,
not all bonds pay 3%, not all mutual funds return 5%,
and not all stocks return 8%; the return estimates
are fictitious, so relax and cut me some slack.

Money in Cheese Budget as of Today:
$ 1,000.00

Year	In **5** Years	In **10** Years	In **20** Years
FDIC insured account 1% APY*	$ 1,051.04	$ 1,104.68	$ 1,220.33
Bonds @ 3% return	$ 1,159.27	$ 1,343.91	$ 1,806.11
Mutual Funds @ 5% return	$ 1,276.28	$ 1,628.89	$ 2,653.29
Stocks @ 8% return	$ 1,469.32	$ 2,158.92	$ 4,660.95

* APY - Annual Percentage Yield

Now let's assume that the price of cheese grows at a modest 2.50% each year, and let's do the same calculation. As of today, he can buy $1,000.00 worth of cheese.

Inflation rate of cheese at : 2.50%

Year	In **5** Years	In **10** Years	In **20** Years
Total cost of $1,000.00 in cheese as of today	$ 1,131.40	$ 1,280.08	$ 1,638.61

In short, to buy what would cost a $1,000.00 in cheese today would cost an additional $638.61 in 20 years.

Now how did make out on their cheese intake? Let's review:

Year	In **5** Years	In **10** Years	In **20** Years
Price of Cheese	$ 1,131.40	$ 1,280.08	$ 1,638.61
FDIC-Insured Account	($ 1,051.04)	($ 1,104.68)	($ 1,220.33)
Uneaten Cheese	($ 80.36)	($ 175.40)	($ 418.28)
Bonds	($ 1,159.27)	($ 1,343.91)	($ 1,806.11)
Cheese Surplus	$ 27.87	$ 63.83	$ 167.50
Mutual Funds	$ 1,276.28	$ 1,628.89	$ 2,653.29
Cheese Surplus	$ 144.88	$ 348.81	$ 1,014.68
Stocks	$ 1,469.32	$ 2,158.92	$ 4,660.95
Cheese Surplus	$ 337.92	$ 878.84	$ 3,022.34

( ) = Negative number

Right out the gate at the 5-year mark, you are already leaving uneaten cheese on the table with a savings account. However, you might think, "You know what, Mel, I can do just fine with $1,220.33 of cheese in 20 years. At least if I put my money into an FDIC insured account, I can't lose my cheese money."

Undoubtedly you can make a killer grilled cheese; however, let's replace cheese with more important things like rent, groceries, healthcare, car insurance, gas for your car, etc. Now think of how much more devastating a shortfall could mean in one of those categories.

Quite frankly, in my industry, we see a lot of people who run the risk of outliving their money. Boomers are healthy; they exercise more than me, they eat better than me, and they will live many long, long years into the future; this unfortunately is why you have 70-year-old people serving your fries. Now add into this the implications of the years of having children, college funds, buying houses, health crises, and retirement years, and you begin to see the long-term implications. See why I say enjoy your money? It is so important.

Also, in this equation, we have not taken into consideration taxes. Each year you are not in a tax-deferred account, Uncle Sam

---

will be taking a portion of your money.

Okay, now that you understand how inflation affects your money, just for funzies, let's see what happens when you take too much money out of your investments too soon. You know, just to really bum you out. In this section of the book, I labored over and over with numbers trying to make them sexy and funny, and quite frankly, you can't dress up a pig.

So here is the best I can do.

According to www.gibson.com there are 10 bands that were recognized at one time or another as the Loudest Rock Bands of all time.

The list is comprised of:

Mötörhead
(a personal favorite),

The Who

MC5

(Kick out the Jams MFer)

AC/DC

(another fav)

My Bloody Valentine

Deep Purple

Led Zepplin

(though not of my generation you can't get hotter than 1970s Robert Plant with his shirt open)

Manowar

Leftfield

KISS

I want to note that I saw Korn in the 90's, and at that time, they were listed as one of the loudest bands. Not sure how or why they didn't make this list. I remember when they started playing *Got the Life*, a pit broke out right where I was sitting on my then boyfriend's shoulders. For those of you who have been in a pit, it can feel dangerous and EXCITING. However, when you are on someone's shoulders AND you are stuck in a pit, believe me it just feels dangerous. God bless that man for having a strong back and great balance! We will transition here to make a complicated subject somewhat entertaining.

Okay, let's say that you are at your favorite band's concert, and they are trying to be one of the Loudest Bands ever. You as a die-hard fan are happy to oblige. Now the concert starts and a bunch of concert goers, hopped up on beer and adrenaline, start screaming their balls off. The concert goers can easily obtain the needed **85+ decibels**.

100% audience   **85 decibels**

However, the band blows harder than your mom, and 25% percent of the crowd gets pissed and leaves.

Now, that 25% of the audience members have left, how much louder would each remaining concert goers have to scream? Did you say 25%? Wrong. They would each have to scream approximately 33% louder to return the concert to the previous decibel reading. The band continues to suck, and now 50% of the people leave.

Each remaining person would have to scream approximately 100% louder than previous to compensate for the concert goers who have left.

The concert progresses, and now 75% of the people have left. How hard would the remaining people have to work to maintain the volume level? Harder than your mom at Hooters two days before pay day. I'm sorry to rank on your mom so much, I'm sure she is a lovely woman and you are lucky to have her. The answer is 300.00% louder than previous, assuming they haven't blown out their vocal cords by then.

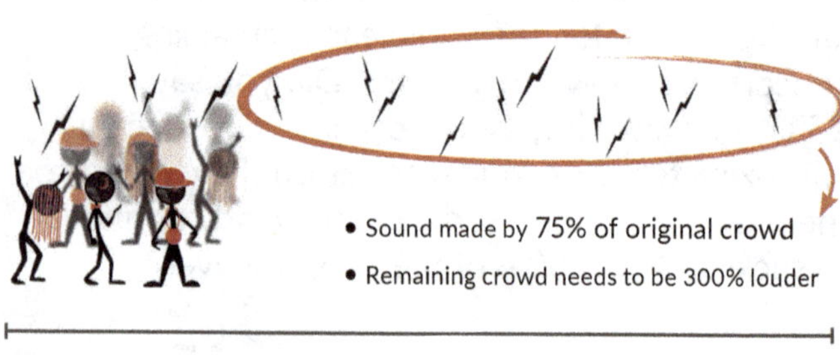

25% audience   **85 decibels**

It's okay, read that paragraph again, and it will start to click.

A quick aside, I saw Warrant years back. Now they were a little too glammy for me, but they were on a multi-act ticket, so I figured why not. Jani Lane was completely wasted. I mean as a long-time concert goer I have seen my share of F'ed up musicians. But Jani Lane-holy shit, he took the cake. When he hit the stage he was so wasted, he repeated the verses twice, stumbled around on stage (not in the charming Ozzy Osbourne way), and missed choruses.

The band was spot on, but halfway into the third song, the crowd rebelled. They booed louder than any crowd of that size I had heard. The fans were jumping up into the spotlight just so the band could see their fans flipping them off. A mass exodus ensued. I think the band eventually had to get off the stage halfway through their set because there was no audience left. I was pissed because I had just purchased a bucket of beers and was not allowed to bring them into the casino, so a chug-a-thon began between my friend and me.

The fiasco was so brilliantly horrible that the casino refunded everyone's money, which never happens. This was especially surprising because Warrant was the last act on the ticket. The next day Warrant played a rock festival and promptly fired Jani. He would die later of alcoholism. According to Bob Seger, *Rock N Roll Never Forgets*, and to date, they are still the worst concert I've ever seen. This event is in fact the basis for this example.

The previous example is a live action instance of what happens when you withdraw too much money too often or too quickly. The dollars remaining (concert goers) have to work harder and harder to keep you at the same level as before you started withdrawing. If inflation is compounding faster than your money, eventually your audience members will drop dead, and you are broke.

Now take that example and imagine a 25-year long concert. How difficult would it be to keep the venue full (or get you through retirement for 25 years)? As a side note, read Stephen King's short story *You Know They Got A Hell of a Band*; it'll tie this up nicely.

Investing is one of the ways that you have an opportunity to outpace inflation aka kick inflation's lilly white ass. Investing doesn't mean taking big risk with your money; like all things there are different levels of risk, and you dictate the amount of risk you are comfortable with. However, in most cases, even a conservative investment (not FDIC insured) will give you the opportunity to outpace inflation.

Playing it safe is not always the right answer. Eventually, you feel inflation, and money that does not outpace inflation does you a disservice, and I call it "dead" money.

90

2008

WTH Happened?

In this chapter:

Blokie

Invests money in
Ponzi scheme first.

Papi D

Buys a mortgage-backed
bond made of sausage ends.

"She works hard for the money / So hard for it, honey / She works hard for the money / So you better treat her right."

- Donna Summers

from **"She Works Hard for the Money'"** off *She Works Hard for the Money* released in 1983

Ozzy

Sells "insurance" (credit default swap) to Papi D.

Slagathor

Moons later, invests money in a Ponzi scheme.

So WTH happened in 2008? In layman's
terms with none of that BS financial jargon.
Indeed. So, let's cover a little of what
happened because 2008 was a shit show.

You know the old saying "No one wants to see how
the sausage is made?" Let's start there. Imagine
you are making sausage (not a great image for my
Jewish bestie), and for each sausage that is made,
you cut off the ends and throw them back into the
grinder. You continue to make sausages, continuing
to cut off the ends and put them back in the
grinder, only taking the choice middle part of the
sausage and packaging them up for sale. Eventually,
because you return the sausage ends back into
the grinder, you have a grinder full of all ends. The
sausage maker, however, has a trusted name and
reputation, so you buy their sausages assuming that
you are getting the choice part of the sausage.

Let's transition here.

Housing prices were going up at a steady clip
from about 2005-2007. As a result, many people
were purchasing houses, and many others were
purchasing additional houses to flip. Mortgages
started out as standard or "prime" mortgages which
required provable income, payments covering
principal (the actual amount borrowed), and

interest, good credit, and a steady job. But as the housing market continued to rise, many mortgage companies (and banks, let's not forget them) got greedy. They began to write mortgages called "sub-prime" mortgages. These were mortgages that didn't need provable income, didn't need the best of credit, weren't concerned with job history or paying down principal, and quite frankly weren't even concerned if you could actually afford the house. Digest that for a minute: you take out a loan and don't have to start paying back what you borrowed. In some cases, negative amortization loans also less than the interest. So again, you are paying no principal back and less than the actual interest accrued on the loan. Seriously, what?!

Many small companies wrote these loans because it produced quick turnover of loan fees, and then the companies being too small to service the loans would turn around and sell the mortgages to bigger banks (they were too big to fail, don't ya know), or in a lot of cases, to Countrywide.

The smaller companies would get an additional profit from the sale of the mortgage then turn around and repeat the process. Now don't fool yourself; the bigger banks were in on the action too, and many (if not all) had "sub-prime" lending divisions as well as practices of buying up outstanding loans from independent mortgage companies or smaller banks. When the smaller mortgage companies went TU, the bigger banks were left holding the bag. This is one of the main reasons the mortgage giant Countrywide went under.

Let's add Step 2 in the process. The big banks—let's call them Bank o 'Merica, Sniti, Bells Hargo, and Face—took these mortgages, packaged them up in funds (see the Mutual Fund Chapter), and sliced them up and sold them to the public. The public bought said slices of funds because the banks' names attached to them were reputable, established, recognizable, and highly rated. The bigger banks sold these slices to investors and earned even more money.

Crappy mortgages go to hell, nice people who bought the slices are left with depreciating values on their shares, and we start a slow slide into recession. Panic breaks out, and the housing market comes crashing down. People start trying to sell their shares, and some get out, and some don't, and chaos ensues.

But wait, there's more...

Credit default swaps. Now, I know you are thinking, "What in the hell are those?" A credit default swap is like having insurance on a fixed income instrument (see the Bond chapter).

What happens is a fun-loving tribesman ⚉ buys a mortgage-backed bond made of sausage ends but, because the name on the package is reputable,

⚉ trusts they are getting choice meats. But just in

case, ⚉ buys "insurance" on the financial instrument to make doubly sure he is paid in the event of a default, and this is called buying a credit default swap.

⚉ purchases a credit default swap from ⚉ .

In return, says that if the fixed income

instrument defaults, he will not only pay back
the premium (the initial price of the instrument) but

also all the interest that was promised to .

 looks at the credit ratings of the issuers of the
fixed income instrument (big banks and financial
houses) and feels the institution won't fail, and they
have limited risk exposure, and feels comfortable

selling the credit default swap. Great racket for
if the fixed income instrument never defaults.

However, if you purchased a mortgage-backed
security from 2007-2009, 9 times out of 10,
you bought a security with all sausage ends.

Then our cycle starts to come full circle.

The housing market grinds to a halt, people walk out
on houses that were way overpriced to begin with,
mortgages default, the investments start collapsing,
the banks start getting hit, and crap keeps rolling
downhill. Our tribe's member is now holding an
instrument that is plunging in value and is defaulting.

 goes to and wants their promised money;

can't pay , and they crash. and are

hosed but mostly.

But wait, there's more...

Preferreds. Remember we discussed preferred stock in an earlier chapter? Well, as a refresher, the point of a preferred stock is to pay a quarterly dividend and, for the most part, maintain its value of around $25.00. Once the financial crisis happened, a lot of companies stopped paying their preferred dividend payments to stock holders. Because of this, preferreds lost value, and some dropped to as low as $5.00. As a preferred stock holder, you are not getting your dividend, and your value is now plummeting.

Think of it this way: a preferred stock that doesn't pay a dividend is like owning a car with no engine—what's the point? This caused more hysteria in the stock market as typically preferred stock holders are more risk adverse than common stock holders to begin with. When a preferred stock starts missing dividends, its credit rating drops, and we continue our descent.

But wait, there's more...

Money Market Funds. These funds are often confused with FDIC-insured products. A true money market fund is not FDIC insured. Prior to 2008, banks liked to confuse you by telling you they had "money market savings accounts"—what a bunch of crap. If the savings account is FDIC insured, then it is not a money market account, plain and simple. But remember we discussed greed? Well, banks knew that people knew that money market funds were known to pay better than regular savings accounts, so they took advantage of people. A true money market fund is comprised of extremely short-term notes that often are not affected by market conditions. Because of this, money market funds have shares, and each slice was worth $1.00, without exception, until 2008. In 2008, all hell was breaking loose, and some of these short-term instruments started to default as a result.

For the first time in money market history, some funds "broke the buck," meaning that the shares fell below $1.00. This was huge because money markets had been believed to be—and in some cases promised to be—safe, and when people fled the stock market, they tended to run right into money market accounts. People used money markets as a cash alternative assuming they would never lose any of their money. Surprise, surprise.

But wait, there's more...

Bernie! No, not Bernie Sanders, Bernie Madoff. The creator and facilitator of one of the largest Ponzi schemes ever. What is that, you ask? Let me explain.

invests money.

Moons later,  invests money.

Moons later,  invests money.

In a Ponzi scheme, there are no "actual" investments.

So  ,  , and  are seeing fictitious statements generated with made-up investments and made-up returns. The facilitator of the scheme,

in this case Bernie Madoff, gives  money to

in the form of made up "returns" and then gives  's

money to  in the form of made up "returns." The client's financial advisor appears to be killing it, and the clients are seeing returns off the charts and watch their balances continue to grow. Greed takes over, and they never question exactly what or how this return is being made or what they are invested in.

This goes on again and again and again. For the most part, this scheme continues to stay afloat as long as there are always more clients with new money coming into the fold and investing. All the while, Bernie Madoff is charging fees for his wonderful management of their money and getting stinking rich. Fuck him. This all works because people don't want to remember "if it looks too good to be true, it probably is."

2008 happens, and people rush madly to their financial advisors to take their money out of the stock market, including Madoff's clients. At this point, the whole process moves in reverse, and eventually the fictitious "returns" and management are exposed. Too many people tried to withdraw their money too close in succession to each other, and with no additional clients and money coming in, they didn't have it, and the house of cards falls. Ka-Blooey!

Sucks, don't it?

But wait there's more...

There is a huge excess of houses on the market, the demand completely falls off, and builders are out of jobs, and people that work for the builders are out of jobs. Industries that support the builders

---

are out of jobs, banks start tightening on lending, and employers need cash flow for payroll and can't get it, so they start to fold, causing more job losses. More people become unemployed, causing them to lose rental properties first then primary homes second. Let us also not forget the crazy spending that had ensued on the lead-up to the housing bubble when everything looked green as hell; those debts are defaulted on as well. Unemployment skyrockets, earnings fall, and we *Tokyo Drift* into the worst economy since the Great Depression, later coined the Great Recession.

Holy crap, I need a drink. To relive that through typing sucks.

Did I cover everything? No. Is there more even I don't understand? Yes. Would an economist explain it better? Yes. Would they be as easy to understand? Doubtful.

So these are a couple key elements that contributed to the perfect storm that was 2008. May you rest in peace and stay there.

With all that said, I still believe in the stock market. Why? Read on...

10

Does the Stock Market Really Blow?

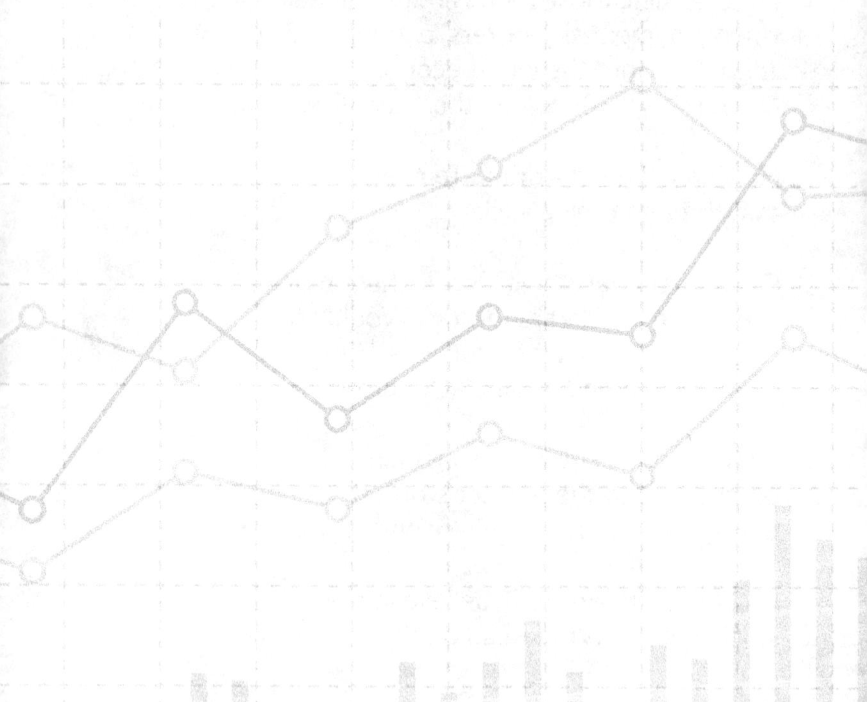

*"Hey broker man please don't make
no more investments / Cause I would
like to keep my shirt and pants"*

- Hank Williams Jr

from **"Stock Market Blues"** off *Old School
New Rules* released in 2012

Interesting to point out that Hank
Williams Jr. is estimated to be worth over
$45,000,000.00. What do you think the
chances are he has no stocks? Slim to none.

Okay, take a deep breath.

I will explain to you what the stock market is,
and you might have to drink a Monster to get
through this chapter, but you'll be so much smarter
afterwards (or, for hipsters, maybe drink a relaxing
chai tea or guava or whatever crap is hip).

Exchanges are the market place for stocks and
other investments. It facilitates the buying and
selling of all types of instruments; think of it like
PayPal but for investments. I want to sell MGM

stock, and you want to buy MGM stock, so we go through a third party known as the New York Stock Exchange (NYSE) or the Nasdaq (NASDAQ) or the Bombay exchange or numerous other exchanges that are all facilitating the buys and sells of particular investments. Now some exchanges are more specialized than others. For instance, the NYSE is broader whereas the NASDAQ is typically a favored exchange for technology companies. However, all stocks are traded on only one exchange. Bill Gates was originally rejected by the NYSE when he was looking for a home for Microsoft, so as a sign of rebellion, he joined NASDAQ and has never left. When we discuss the investments in the stock market, we are referring to non-FDIC insured products, sometimes referred to as securities or equities. Exchanges are huge playgrounds for stocks and other investment vehicles, but everyone stays in their own playground.

Exchanges are too extensive to try to track all the investments in their playground, and there is really no way of telling who is doing well and who is not. So here enters our measuring stick, the indexes: the Dow Jones 30 (the Dow) and the S&P 500 (the S&P). Now there are tons of other indexes, but we will keep it simple here. The S&P is made up of 500 US companies whereas the Dow is made up of 30 US companies. When people refer to the market being up or down, they are usually speaking about one of these indexes. The indexes are designed as an attempt to track all the investments in the exchanges' playgrounds. Think of it as the speed limit of the market. If these indexes are moving higher, usually that means the overall market is also moving higher. Depending on the exchange, sometimes you can quickly know what sectors had good days or bad. As mentioned above, the NASDAQ is a favored exchange for the tech companies, so if the NASDAQ is down, typically the technology sector will be having a down day overall.

Now, you need to be careful when following an index and drawing a direct correlation to your portfolio. Oftentimes people will see the DOW down and call me assuming that that means their portfolio is down also. Not always the case. You see, most indexes are weighted. Which means that each stock in the index isn't represented equally.

Let me explain. As mentioned above, the DOW is only 30 US companies. However, the DOW is also weighted based on stock price. So, for instance, at the time of this writing, the highest priced stock in the DOW is Boeing (BA) at around $327.00 per share while the lowest priced stock is General Electric (GE) at around $14.00. All the stocks are added up and divided by 30, so therefore the stocks with the highest share price carry the most weight. As it stands now, if BA has a really bad day, it will drag down the DOW even if the majority of the other stocks were up. In order to get the same correlated returns as the DOW, you would need to hold all 30 stocks weighted the exact same way and ONLY those 30 stocks from the DOW. It still won't be exact, but that is as close as you can get.

The S&P is also weighted but in a different manner. The S&P uses the price per share as a factor, but then it multiples that share price by the outstanding shares (see Stock chapter). Again, larger companies with more shares outstanding AND higher stock prices can sway the S&P in the same manner as stock price can sway the DOW. However, with a total of 500 different companies, it is a little harder to do. That is why most people use the S&P 500 as a better indicator than the DOW.

To break it down, when you invest in the stock market, you are typically buying stocks and/ or mutual funds which are the most common investments. So your mutual fund is traded on an exchange (NYSE) that probably contains stocks in it that are tracked by an index like the S&P and are held in your 401k or investment account. Holy crap, I could go for some cheese about now.

While investments in the stock market can fluctuate and lose value, they also give you the best chance to retire early, travel more, buy that sports car, be philanthropic, buy a Shih Tzu, beat inflation, or whatever you're into. As discussed in previous chapters, having safe money doesn't guarantee that the long-term effects of inflation and taxes will not be damaging to your future or current lifestyle. In my opinion, inflation is the silent killer, and playing it too safe in the end will be a losing proposition, especially with people living so long nowadays. So my point is this: invest for your goals. Lots of people in my industry want to tell you about the portfolio they are going to build for you or how they have got the "one thing" different from all of us that they do. Guys, we're all buying the same shit for the most part. But if you know what your objective is, then a professional can help put you in the right investments that balance your risk tolerance with fulfillment of your dreams. Being afraid isn't resolving anything; chase your dreams, understand the jargon, and have less fear.

Also—shameless plug—working with a CFP® helps; did I mention I am a CFP?

11

Behavioral Finances

Why you shouldn't trust your emotions

*"They'll hear you say / I'm a comin' your way /
And I'm only just a growin' / A little each day"*

\- The Doobie Brothers

from **"Growin' a Little Each Day"** off ***The
Doobie Brothers*** released in 1971

Buy low/Sell high

"Buy low, sell high." If you know nothing about investing, you know this, and you tell me, FREQUENTLY, especially if you're a drunk guy in a bar trying to impress me with your overwhelming investment knowledge. You see, everyone has heard that mantra, but few people understand it or have the will power to do just that when the market is tumbling. Lucky for us, we have a tool known as dollar-cost averaging (DCA) to help. DCA is something most people do and don't realize they're doing it or the power it holds. When you put money in a 401k every month, you are dollar-cost averaging little by little each month, regardless of market conditions, slow and steady. Now during 2008, I heard a ton of people tell me they stopped

---

putting money in their 401ks because their balance just kept going down. D'oh! That is the worst thing you could do. Do you think Warren Buffet, the Oracle from Omaha, is a billionaire because he bought high? Hell no! As each month's contribution goes into your account, you are constantly picking up shares; the cheaper the shares, the more of them you purchase, like shoes at Nordstrom's half yearly sale. Instead of one pair for $100.00, you can get two pairs and a cute necklace.

Let's look at an example:

Let's assume every month you put $100.00 into an investment, regardless of market conditions. In other words, you dollar cost average (DCA).

Month	Share Price	Investment	Number of Shares purchased
1	$ 50.00	$ 100.00	2
2	$ 50.00	$ 100.00	2
3	$ 25.00	$ 100.00	4
4	$ 50.00	$ 100.00	2

Now assume you would have sold everything
at the end of the fourth month, and let's
look at the profitability of each month.

Shares purchased in month 1 at the end
of month 4 gain in value $0.00.

Shares purchased in month 2 at the end
of month 4 gain in value $0.00.

Shares purchased in month 3 at the end
of month 4 gain in value $100.00.

Shares purchased in month 4 at the end
of month 4 gain in value $0.00.

At the end of month 4, you had a total number of
10 shares of the choice investment. However, the
only shares to make you money would be the ones
purchased in month 3 when the market had dropped.

To reiterate, you made money when the market
dropped thus "buying low, selling high." You see,
many people lament 2008, and let's be clear, it
sucked out loud, but there was a lot of money made
from purchases during that time. If you are forever
in a market where the stock price is increasing, then
you severely limit your chance to make good stable
gains. DCA can also be used to ease slowly back

into a recovering market as well as to take advantage of dips. The main thing that DCA accomplishes is the ability to take the emotions out of investing. Often people let their emotions lead, but this can be devastating. Next to sex and politics, nothing is more personal than your money. Unfortunately, I still have the toughest time getting clients into a declining market. Fear takes over, and this is known as behavioral finance. And most times, behavioral finance equals death (financial death, you know what I'm saying). So save the emotions for your loved ones, and don't scroll past without typing "AMEN."

12

The Taxman Cometh

*"You know you want to mack this / Because
I come stronger than the IRS / Whenever
you done got delinquent on your taxes"*

- DJ Quik

from **"Let's Get Down"** off ***Tony! Toni! Toné!*** released in 1996

There was a quote once attributed to P Diddy
(Puff Daddy, Diddy, or Sean Combs, depending
on your age group) that stated something to the
effect that he was proud to pay almost 50% in
taxes. Well, screw that. If he wants to pay so much
in taxes, I will be glad to give him my tax bill.

For most normal people, taxes are C Blockers.
If inflation is the silent killer, taxes hold you
at gun point and kick you in the nads. Ha,
nads! Sorry, just made myself laugh again.

Taxes are blatant; they are forever on every
politician's lips, raising or lowering, restricting,
understanding, etc. Hats off to my CPAs
(Certified Public Accountants) out there. Better
you than me dealing with that crap. However,

you need to understand how taxes work, how to tax defer money, how to pay less taxes if possible, etc. The easiest way to defer taxes is through Individual Retirement Accounts (IRA) and 401ks. IRAs like a 401k is not the investment; it's the vehicle. So here is a quick rundown comparing a Roth IRA and a traditional IRA.

**My numbers are not meant to be used for tax purposes; they are to be used for example only, so don't be foolish and check with your tax advisor for specifics.

	IRA/401k	ROTH IRA
Annual Assumed Income	$ 100,000.00	$ 100,000.00
Contribution	$ 5,000.00	$ 5,000.00
Taxable income for contribution year	$ 95,000.00	$ 100,000.00
Contribution amount	$ 5,000.00	$ 5,000.00
Grows over years by	$ 5,000.00	$ 5,000.00
Total Account Value	$ 10,000.00	$ 10,000.00
Tax Treatment on withdrawal after age 59.5	$ 10,000.00 100% Taxable	$ 10,000.00 100% Tax Free
Summary	Save taxes now, pay them later	Pay taxes now, save them later

Do you see what happened there? With an IRA
or 401k, you get a tax break today. The additional
$5,000.00 in growth grows tax deferred, but
when the money is withdrawn after age of 59.5,
it is 100% taxable to you at whatever ordinary
income rates are at that time. When you contribute
to a ROTH IRA, there is no tax break today and
the additional $5,000.00 in growth grows tax
deferred, and when the money is withdrawn
after age of 59.5, it is tax-free (no taxes).

Before we continue, WTH is tax deferred?

Tax deferred means that as the money grew
in the account, you were not charged taxes
on it, and the taxes were deferred to some
point in the future. If an account is designed
for retirement, it will offer you tax deferral on
the growth. A Roth IRA or a traditional IRA
will determine how much is tax deferred.

To belabor the point, if you invest in a savings
account and it earns you $200.00 in interest,
in the year the interest was earned, you will
be taxed on the full $200.00. If those same
$200.00 were earned in an IRA, you would
not be taxed on the $200.00 because the IRA
allows for tax deferral on the growth. Get it?

An important side note about Roth IRAs is that they have an additional 5-year holding period requirement. If you pull the money out of the Roth before 5 years, unless it's under special circumstances, you will pay additional penalties. If you are 23 years of age and you put money into a Roth and pull it out after or at the age of 59.5, you will have satisfied your 5-year waiting period. This period starts the day the Roth IRA is established, so if you are 60 and you open a Roth IRA, you will need to wait an additional 5 years.

Regarding 401ks, some companies out there provide matching opportunities for dollars contributed into a 401k. Basically, the company is giving you a free match of money. If you are fortunate enough to have a company match, you owe it to yourself to take FULL advantage of that match. If they match to 10%, then damnit, you put in 10%. To leave that money on the table is foolish at the least. Also, for every $1.00 you put in your 401k, it is not an equivalent to a dollar missing from your paycheck. Depending on your tax bracket, it could be more like for every $1.00 you invest in you 401k, it is the equivalent of only missing $0.70 out of your paycheck.

Clear as mud?

Great, Mel, but get to the point. Which should I do? Typical rule of thumb is if you are under age 40, Roth IRA, and if you are over age 40, traditional IRA. But this is the deal: it depends on you and your goals. All your investments should be catered to your goals. It depends on things like your current tax situation and how soon you will use the money. The one standard rule with IRAs is this: do not put money in an IRA or 401k if you will need to access that money before the age of 59.5. IRAs are not designed to be touched before then.

13

Budgeting...

and Why You Should Love It

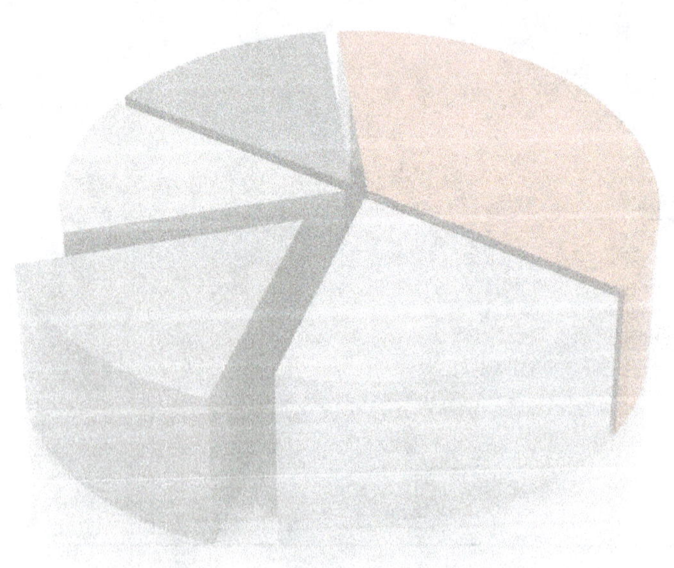

"So young and so naïve, I thought it would be easy / But now I know I've got to take / Control".

- Janet Jackson

from **"Control"** off *Control* released in 1986

First of all, let me tell you from experience, my own and others, that **your finances are just as fucked up as everyone else's**. Sorry for the F bomb, but I need to make this point clear so it sticks in your mind.

Clients will tell me about affairs and all kinds of stuff and then apologize for their finances being messed up. It's okay. You are NORMAL. Besides, I am assuming you are reading this book to improve, no? So go easy on yourself and save being self-conscious for your looks or whatever else traumatizes you.

Great, Mel, but you forgot one thing: I don't have money to invest or contribute to a 401k/IRA or my other financial goals.

Enter our friend, the "Budget."

Nothing brings sickness in your throat like the word "budget." It sounds like the crappiest place on Earth to be in/on a budget, the anti-Disneyland. Let's stop looking at a budget as a bad thing, and let's start looking at it as budgeting for the good stuff.

Now some people might not be concerned with retirement or buying a house or owning the hottest new car. The cool thing is that whatever you're interested in (good cheese), a budget will help you get there. Money is not just money; I want to murder people's faces when I hear them say, "It's only money." Let's put aside the fact that we are the richest country in the world (currently) and that tons of Americans are homeless and realize that every dollar you earn represents time out of your life you gave up earning that dollar. We can speak of the rewards of a hard day's work, but one thing I have consistently heard from clients is that if they could do anything but work, that would be preferable. So this is how a budget can help you.

Let's assume you make $10.00 an hour working. You have exchanged your time doing something fun to earn that $10.00 working. If you then turn around and give Starbucks $5.00 of it for coffee, you just squandered 30 minutes of your life for a caffeine fix. Look man, I get it. I am a diet (anything) cola junky. I am not saying you shouldn't enjoy your money (says the woman who has seen Mötley Crüe 17 times)—quite the opposite. I just want you to budget for it. So if you know you're a Starbucks addict, then budget for your coffee consumption. Budget to bring more enjoyment into your life, cut out the useless crap you spend money on, and plan for the good stuff. If having a Starbucks every day is where your joy is found, then that is one of your financial objectives. However, if going to Italy is your financial objective, maybe drink coffee from home.

Guidelines for typical monthly budgeting earned income are as follows:

5%-10%	Savings
Max of 30%	Rent/Mortgage
Max of 20%	Utilities (phone, power, water, garbage, etc.)
Max of 15%	Debt Payments (student loans, credit cards, etc.)
Max of 10%	Dining/Entertainment/Travel
Max of 15%	Groceries

I know child care, pet care, medical care, and insurance is not listed here, and they are all important. This is just to give you the most basic of ideas of what you should shoot for (obviously without percentages exceeding 100%). Now, the wonderful part about this is that the numbers are pliable; they're your numbers, so they are whatever you say they are. If you pay no rent or mortgage, great! You just found up to 30% of your income you can use to spread amongst the other expenses, or you can add some items not listed above.

If you tell me that you do not have enough money every month, then that tells me you are living on credit or savings. Look man, we've all done it. But are the things you are buying while pulling your money down from savings and credit for necessary items? Not coffee at Starbucks but food on your table? If the answer is no, then you've got some work to do. It won't be fun, at first, but eventually this really weird thing happens where you become obsessed with your numbers.

When I was younger, I would look at my account and have about $5.48 left after expenses. If I needed gas (pre-debit card era), I would have to drive to the only cash machine that allowed you to take out money in increments of $5.00. Back then, I called (yes, guys, this was before the internet) and checked my balance everyday, even if the balance was only $5.48, because it was MY $5.48, and once you lay claim to your money, you are taking back your time. Let me reiterate, **once you lay claim to your money, you are taking back your time.** Do not underestimate the power of this statement.

Now, let's discuss two common errors made when creating/running a budget.

The first is self-punishment. Budgets are not designed to be rigid, and oftentimes if you spend more in one category of budgeting thus going overbudget, it can make you feel like a failure. Let's look at what I mean.

Let's say you make $100.00 per month, and you have two budget categories: Dining Out and Entertainment, both allotted with $50.00 each. A band you love comes to town, and their tickets cost $75.00. You want to go see them, so you buy the ticket. Now, obviously, you have just spent $75.00 on "Entertainment" and have exceeded your allotted entertainment budget by $25.00. Did you screw up your month? NO, you just spend only $25.00 on Dining Out for that month to compensate for your $25.00 overage in the Entertainment budget. It's not the end of the world; it's just something cool happened that month that normally doesn't.

The second is lying to yourself and not taking the time to correctly track your expenses. Let me give you an example that I had to break myself of doing.

As previously stated I am a diet cola junkie. Anytime I get gas, I always go into the store to see if my favorite diet soda is on sale. Usually, I can get two 22ozers for $2.50, so a lot of times my gas receipt will show $27.50 ($25.00 in gas plus $2.50 in diet soda). Here is where you need to have self-control. If you are truly budgeting correctly, you would show $25.00 out of your gas budget and $2.50 out of your grocery budget, not $27.50 out of your gas budget or whatever budget item has the most money left in it. It's like cheating at golf; it never gets you ahead, and you never can see how far you've come. Another version of this is going grocery shopping and pulling cash out to go drinking with. NOPE, that does not come out of your grocery budget. Allocate it correctly, and don't screw yourself.

When budgeting, your aim is to set up a budget for your monthly income. If you are super organized and you have annual expenses like car tags, you can be ahead of the game by doing a budget three months at a time. However, the overall budget is for total monthly income WITH a mandatory savings factor of 5%-10%. After that, you start with fixed bills: rent, mortgage, car insurance, loan payments, child care, etc. Then non-discretionary variable expenses like utilities, groceries, and gas. Then, with the remaining money, you plan for fun stuff. Concerts, dining out, movies, etc.

Now, as you are moving through your month, the money that goes into savings should go into an FDIC insured savings account, and this is known as your emergency fund. Emergency funds have two purposes. The most important is to replace all your expenses (bills & lifestyle) for a certain period of months in the event of job loss or something catastrophic. General rule of thumb is that in a household where two people are working, you would need to set aside 3 months of expenses. If you are a sole income earner in a household, then 6 months of expenses is your target. Once you have achieved this, you can keep saving if you'd like.

Is there such a thing as too much savings? Well, yes, actually. Once you hit your monthly reserve and add a little cushion for the pushin', you should really avert your monthly savings to other things. These dollars could be set aside for a financial objective, paying down debt, or to be put into an investment vehicle as a way to seek possible higher returns. Please do not do what I see so many people do; they sit with HUGE balances in their savings accounts. For what?! That money is what I call "dead money" in the fact that it usually earns little interest, is taxable, and doesn't beat inflation.

Life is short, guys; shit happens. Please be smart, but don't be afraid to enjoy your money!

To close this out, a lot of people think that paying their bills and then spending the rest of their money is budgeting. Wrong! That's just paying your bills. Once you start budgeting, it will become clear what the most enjoyable things are to you, and by becoming aware of this by default, you will focus more on those things. Once you start looking at your money as a symbol for your time, it will change your thoughts on money. Seriously, it will mess with your head, and it's permanent. You're welcome.

Once you understand how budgeting works, share it with your friends. Help me help you help them, or be a stand-up guy and buy him/her a copy of this book.

A Word in Edgewise

We have covered a lot in the book, and if you've made it here, you should feel accomplished right now. I know that money and especially investments can seem scary and boring, but you powered through. Anything new is scary. Hell, I am still afraid to rollerblade because I have little bird ankles. I can avoid rollerblading my whole life; YOU cannot avoid understanding money. Quite frankly, why would you? You need it, I need it, and everyone in your life needs it. Before you read another financial book, stop and make sure you have a budget in place.

At the absolute minimum, know where you're spending your money. I guarantee you are spending more than you think on what you choose to spend it on. If you build proper habits now, at some point in the future, you will be killing it and not even realize it! I have a vested interest in your success. You are part of my global community as well as future clients of mine and members of the Hot Moon Tribe. More importantly, I need you to get out there and create: create your music, your happiness, your travels, and your memories. We are all part of the same energy, and your future is as important to me as mine should be to you.

Here's what I'd ask. With the purchase of this book, 10% of the net profits benefits one of the non-profits below:

1. Forgotten Not Gone
    (https://forgottennotgone.org/)
    An organization helping to prevent veteran suicide

2. Hearts Alive Village
    (https://www.heartsalivevillage.org/)
    To nurture a compassionate society where pets are supported in their homes and on their journey to find a home.

So if you can buy another copy of this book
to give to a friend, please do and help support
these non-profits. If you truly do not have any
more money to purchase another book, then
get a budget and give this copy to a friend to
read and help them understand money.

We have got to do better with our money, all of us.

I BELIEVE IN YOU!

Rock On- Mel O CFP® / Rocker Chick Extraordinaire

P.S. If you'd like to create good karma, reach out to
the non-profits directly and donate a couple dollars.

For kick-ass Slagathor, Ozzy, Papi D, and Blokie
merchandise, check us out at
financestheotherfword.com

To contact Mel O directly for speaking engagement
or consultation, email her at
mel@financestheotherfword.com

#FTOFWpod #FOFWpod #financestheotherfword

Acknowledgments

FINANCES. The Other "F" Word

I would like to acknowledge the people without whom this book would never have been written. Thank you for your support and input.

First, to my mother Becky and my father John.
Anne Bobincheck
Darrell Evans
Derrick Reynolds
Ed Capiral
Gwendolyn Plano
Jax Scott
Jennifer Shook
Joyce Hicks-Reynolds
Linda Little
Lisa Ariola
Marianne Allen
Michelle Nissan
Olivia Gomez
Sandra Andrews
Stormie Andrews
Stephani Ortiz
Zoe Terry

9 781733 665926